Near Myths

Papa Stylianos . . . who taught me to drink 'monkishly'

John Ebdon
NEAR MYTHS
A Love Affair with Greece

David & Charles
Newton Abbot   London

British Library Cataloguing in Publication Data

Ebdon, John, 1923-
Near myths.
1. Greece. Description & travel
I. Title
914.95'0476

ISBN 0-7153-9043-0

Printed in Great Britain
by Billings and Sons   Worcester
for David & Charles Publishers plc
Brunel House   Newton Abbot   Devon

Contents

To

My many friends in the scattered chips of the Greek
islands and particularly to Papa Stylianos of Paleochora
in Crete who taught me to drink 'monkishly'; and to
Maria who looked on indulgently.

Introduction

As with my previous books this one is no tourist guide to the Greek islands. Primarily it is about people – the indigenous and the tourists who one way and another have enriched my life by entering it. Within these pages you will find tears and laughter, love and hate, pathos and bathos – a mixture which is the very ethos of Greece and her people.

Greece is changing: politically, economically, socially; and by the time these words appear in print the picture I have painted may have been altered radically. But, as I have written, no matter how she ages and changes I shall always adore her for she is my Mistress; and with her I hope to end my days.

1
Romiosini

Excluding the thoughts of enjoying luxuries such as a good bottle of wine innocent of resination, of addressing myself to a meal still excited by the heat of the oven which gave birth to its offering, and of the ineffable joy of sitting comfortably upon a lavatory seat without fear of having my buttocks tweaked not once, but thrice by cracked green plastic seemingly endowed with a life of its own, I never look forward to leaving the islands of Greece and returning to the mourning skies of Britain and the lugubrious aura of the London borough of Brent. Invariably I find the transition traumatic, frequently mope for days and, like Job of the Old Testament, refuse to be comforted. It is then that I turn to a desk drawer in my study filled with a miscellany of bric-à-brac from Greece.

Therein lies an amber *kombouloi*, the worry beads given to me by one Papa Stylianos, a great-hearted if sexually orientated seventy-year-old priest from Paleochora in south-western Crete; a red painted Paschal pullet's egg from a long-past Easter on the island of Kos, decorated on one side with a vine leaf and adorned on the other with the sign of the cross; there is a terracotta-veined shell from Karpathos in the Dodecanese; a christening doll still pregnant with stale sugared almonds – a memento from a Rhodian village; a petrified twig plucked from the volcano's rim on the isle of Nisyros formed, so legend has it, by a cliff-top torn from Kos by the god Poseidon and hurled across the sea to bury Polybutes in the Battle of the Giants; and a cheap key ring given to my long time friend Maria by a fisherman on Simi.

Collectively their intrinsic value is negligible but every item is a gem to me. Each is a memory bank which opens when I touch it, the anthithesis of Pandora's urn, and once again I feel the pulse of Greece and hear the heartbeat of the islands.

Back come the remembrances: of scents of oregano, thyme and other wild herbs in purple hills, and Greek tobacco smoke and garlic; of sounds of cicadas and braying mules, of the strains of the plaintive *lyra* and ubiquitous bouzoukis; and of days, glorious mercurial days, of deep emotion and high elation when laughter swiftly turned to tears which just as quickly dried. A pot-pourri of memories which spells one word to me – Greekness, – or, as they would say, *romiosini*.

The Greeks may have a word for it but having invented *romiosini* none, in my experience, can define Greekness in a sentence. This inability is not surprising. The Greek character is as complex and rich as the language itself and initially just as difficult to fathom. Personally I would describe Greekness as being larger than life, an innate ability to conjure dramatic bricks from very little straw and with an ease which makes Euripides appear as a tyro, a firmly held belief that time is only an idea in the mind of God, and a hypochondriacal concern for one's health. No Greek worthy of his or her salt will admit to being wholly free of some ailment, real or imaginary, and conversation on the topic is to them what the weather is to the British. Add to this mixture the love of argument and rhetoric, pride, fierce individuality and a zest for life – and nowhere are these traits better exampled than in the hill villages of Crete – then Greekness begins to be understood. But that is only the beginning of the analysis: there are other ingredients.

Greekness means showing one's emotions at all times, and in all places. In Greece, bathos and pathos go hand in hand: both sadness and joy are expressed with equal vehemence. When a Greek mourns he does so uninhibitedly: at a Grecian wake even the coffee is black. And in the islands at Easter, that festival of festivals in Greece, before the proclamation of the risen Christ is celebrated in churches ablaze with candelabras and brilliant with all the rich pageantry of Greek Orthodoxy, when the air is heavy with incense and passion and the cries of '*Christos anesti!* Christ is risen!' reach the stars and the night

. . . an innate ability to conjure bricks from very little straw . . .

11

erupts with fireworks, the days are filled with extravagant melancholy and the feet of the dancers are stilled. But when a Greek turns his back on death and embraces life he does so hugely, for then he is her lover. As a wise old man from the island of Siphnos in the Cyclades once told me: 'You see Yanni, when a Greek is born, he *follows* life. And then, he *fights* life – and *wins* it. And then Yanni, he *enjoys* life! *Endaxi?* O.K.? *Bravo!* And *that*, Yanni, is *romiosini!*'

That grizzled old sage's appreciation was sound in every aspect. The Greeks have always had to battle with life. From the time of the Persian invaders to the civil war in 1946, the scars of which are still festering in public life today, the whole of their history – as rugged and fragmented as their landscape – endorses this fact; but Stavros, for that was his name, omitted one characteristic from his catalogue: *perieryeea'* – curiosity. Like Kipling's 'Elephant Child' the Greek islander is filled with 'satiable curtiosity'. This too is a firmly entrenched idiosyncrasy of the Greeks, another facet of their personality which has not changed since ancient times. Witness, for example, the confrontation and interrogation of Athena by Odysseus's son Telemachius in Homer's *Odyssey*: 'Do tell me, who are you? From where do you come, what is your native town – who are your people? And since you have not come on foot, what vessel brought you here? Then there is another thing . . .'

The format remains to this day. At an initial meeting with an indigenous member of a Greek village the visitor will face as searching a cross-examination of his personal history, often including demands for a detailed account of his more intimate life-style, as that to which he would be subjected if applying for admission to a pension scheme orientated toward the over-fifties by the Scottish Amicable Life Assurance Society. Presuming that the interrogator has a knowledge of one's mother tongue or that the person questioned is capable of speaking basic Greek, on contemporary lines, a rough translation of such a conversation might run as follows:

'*Yasas phile mou* – blessings my friend! *Ti kanete* – how are you? You are? Ah good! Unfortunately I am not. *Oche! Oche!* No!

No! I have a pain you understand. *Ne* – yes. In my stomach, *ne*. Yesterday it was in my backside, *ne* in the bottom; and tomorrow the God knows where it will be. But never mind, *ine e zoi* – that is life. Ha! Ha! *Alla tora pestemou parakalo?* But now, tell me please, what is your name? Really? Well! Well! Well! Fancy that! I'm a Yanni too! And from where do you come? Ah, *Londino!* My wife's second cousin lives in London. *Ne*, in Kilburn. *Ne*, his name is Apostolis – perhaps you know him. He is a waiter in a *taverna* called Anaemos I think . . . No? Well, *thenbirazi* – it does not matter. Anyway, how old are you, what do you do, how much do you earn, and how many children have you? Two boys and a girl? Ah, *bravo! Bravo!* Well done! Alas I have none. *Oche! Tipota* – nothing. It is not my fault you understand. *Oche* – it is my wife's. she is barren you understand. *Ne* barren, barren, barren. Three times she has made the pilgrimage up Mount Zambikia on her knees, *ne*, to the very summit, to the priest at the top. Her grandmother told her it would work as it had for her, but nothing has happened. Now she is thinking about test tubes, *ne*. But tell me, what do *you* think about test tubes? And the Margaret Thatcher? And . . .' and so on and so on or, as they would say, *ke talipa ke talipa*. And aeons away, shrouded in the mists of time, old Homer smiles contentedly. His laws are being proliferated, the old customs continued, and could he but hear, he would be proud of his children.

So too would Plato of blessed memory; his edicts are also honoured.

Plato was a remarkable citizen. Not only a splendid writer of verse, drama and author of *The Republic,* a work based on the conception of an ideal state ruled directly by moral philosophers and one later to be criticised roundly by Aristotle and others with the vigour of SDP supporters attacking a Labour manifesto, he was probably the first Athenian to acknowledge the importance of the tourist industry to Greece. Unknowingly, but as long ago as 350BC and with extraordinary foresight in Book 12 of the *Laws,* his last and longest sermon to the world, offering the concept of an ideal community in

13

Crete rejoicing in the unattractive name of Magnesia, which
to modern ears suggests a laxative rather than a Utopian
state, he apprised the present Greek Tourist Organisation
of the attraction of their country to the overseas visitor and,
moreover, pigeon-holed their strata. "There are", he wrote,

> four categories of foreign visitors. Those in the first
> turn up every year without fail, usually in summer,
> with the regularity of migratory birds. Most of them
> are on business trips in search of profit, and through-
> out the summer they wing their ways . . . across the
> seas to foreign parts. These visitors must be received
> when they come to the city, at the markets, harbours
> and public buildings outside the city by the officials in
> charge thereof; *and they shall have a care lest any visitors
> introduce any innovation* . . .

Unfortunately for Plato's peace of mind – and the italics
are mine – this last piece of intelligence was largely ignored,
hence the introduction of McDonald's hamburgers in Athens,
the presence of genuine Greek wiener schnitzel in Rhodes,
pina coladas complete with miniature parasols and sparklers
in Kos, and the sale of candy floss in developing island
coastal villages.

Plato would not have been pleased by these developments.
'Change,' he would have reiterated sorrowfully, his finger
pointing sternly to Law No. 797, 'except in something evil,
is extremely dangerous.' However, despite this lapse, and in
accordance with his other decrees, those precursors of our present-day representatives of package tours, travel agencies and
exporters of fast food were received with kindness, as they are
today. So too were the other varieties of visitants enumerated
by Plato and generally classified as sightseers. 'All', said he,

> must be attended to; duly honoured as a friend with
> tokens of esteem . . . these are the laws that should
> govern the reception of all our visitors from abroad –

of either sex. We must show respect for Zeus the god of Strangers, and not keep aliens at arm's length by uncongenial food.

Not all excursionists to Greece would agree that Plato's last injunction has been taken to heart; listening to a disgruntled sextet at Rhodes airport morosely waiting for their charter flight back to England after a twelve-day sojourn in a neon-lit and brash hotel in the centre of that city's tourist cauldron I was left in no doubt of that. Denied their homeland comforts of hot chips, wet fish, real ale and pots of tea they were an unhappy company impatient for their native Scunthorpe, who avowed *en masse* that never again would they repeat their Grecian experience and that next year they would be returning to Torremolinos where, as on previous visits, their daily requirements would be met and, moreover, their bel-loved English understood. Squid, they proclaimed loudly to a captive audience in the stiffling departure lounge alive with calamine-coated grizzling children, had no appeal for them, stuffed or battered; and cuttlefish was only fit for budgies. As for the portions . . .

Greece is changing: tourism is now a major part of her economy. And, sad to say, it is true that in many of her cities and towns frequented by tourists in search of high sun, low overheads and little else – the majority take 'Greekness' to mean just that, having no wish for involvement with the Greeks, let alone their language – the visitors' worth is evalu-ated in drachmae regardless of their nationality. Nor does the boorish behaviour of a small but vociferous minority showing scant respect for their host nation's traditions enhance their reputation. Consequently *philoxenia*, the hospitality as under-stood by Plato, now has to be hunted out like a flea unless one is *persona grata* in the tiny *tavernas* in little back streets where only Greek is spoken, where the air is thick with cigarette smoke and the smell of garlic and oregano, and the sounds of the *rembetika*, the haunting blues from the barren uplands of Anatolia of long ago – the alluring love songs spiced with sexual innuendo and the perversity of fate, sung and plucked from bouzoukoi and *baglamas* – are heard, and where men dance together on table tops and crash their heads together in ecstasy. 'Oooh pah!' they cry or expel their breath through clenched front teeth with a Thh! Thh! Thh!, call for another bottle of retsina, and embrace you as one of theirs and then send you on your way with a gift of sweet *vasilico*, the soft-scented herb basil which clings to one's clothing and lingers as a reminder of long farewells.

It is behind such dingy doors in ill-lit alleys where the bat-eared, long-tailed raffish cats of Greece – surely descendants of the guardians of Egyptian tombs – prowl, fight, caterwaul and copulate until the dawn spells *finis* to their nocturnal pleasures and they slink away to lick their wounds or contemplate their conquests, that *philoxenia* is still to be found. And that intrinsic element which is so much a part of the ethos of Greece remains alive in the 'undiscovered' hill and coastal villages of the Greek islands. In such places obeisance is still paid to *Xenios* Zeus, the god of hospitality, and as in the old Greek language the words stranger and guest remain synonymous. There one is greeted, as Maria and I have been, in simple *cafe neons* with a '*Kalos! Kalos!* Welcome! Welcome!' from its shuffling, often arthritic black-beshawled incumbent to be offered ice-cold spring water as fresh as life itself, preserved soft fruits steeped in syrup – apricots, cherries, figs and loquats – sweet black coffee served in small coarse cups and then sent on our way with a '*Sto kalo!* Go to the good! But come back! Come back – there is so much to talk about! Indeed, why do you not stay? For a week perhaps? Or more? *Ne? Thia na perasome tin ora, katalavis?* To pass the time, you understand?' . . .

Such memories are precious and will never be erased. No more will the remembrances of the two of us sitting with a goatherd heavy with the smell of his charges on the lower slopes of a hill below Antimachia in Kos and sharing with him his midday meal of bitter, dried black olives, rank cheese and *paximathia*, the rock-hard, twice-baked dark-brown bread which he smashed against a nearby stone and then dunked

16

. . . long-tailed, bat-eared raffish cats . . .

the segments into a billy-can of thin red wine made from his own grapes until they softened. *'Kali oreksi,'* he said, 'good appetite,' and crossed himself three times from right to left, opened his mouth to receive the offering and smiled a happy toothless smile as the purple juice trickled down his stubbled chin. *'Ine kala, ne?'* he inquired through the half-eaten bread, 'it is good, yes?' *'Poli kala,'* we agreed, 'very good,' and swilled our own mouthfuls down with more wine from the communal can, as insects hummed in nearby olive groves and in the distance goat bells tinkled faintly from around the necks of the grazing herd below.

Nor will I forget an early morning in a hill village in south-western Crete when the mists still hugged the valleys and hollows and where, before the sun had peaked the surrounding mountain tops, our day began with libations of *tsikouthia*, the Cretan raki, a fiery, transparent liquid made from a distillation of grape skins and stalks left over from the pressing of the wine which is drunk like schnapps, in a single gulp, and without which no Cretan mountain villager will willingly face the middle hours. It has the kick of a mule and sends the blood a-racing through the veins. Three times in quick succession Andonis, our farmer host, recharged our glasses and thrice our stomachs were set ablaze. *'Panda harumene!'* we cried to each other as we downed the liquid fire, *'harumene panda!* Always joy and joy for ever!' *'Ne!'* roared Andonis, a blue-eyed moustached giant of seventy years with a brick-red face and scarred thick hairy arms, *'ke panda irene!* And peace for ever!' And crashing his empty glass upon the rough wooden courtyard table, immediately replenished it. 'One more,' he said. *'thia na skotosome to microvio –* just to kill the microbe!' And he winked.

'Po! Po! Po!' said his wife Anatasia, full-bosomed, dark and dumpy as she brought us a plate of freshly picked fruit from the overhanging branches of an apricot tree. 'He drinks too much! But there it is! *Ti thakanome* – what can we do?' And laughing indulgently and shaking her head she threw up her hands and moved slowly toward her open kitchen door followed by two chickens and a moulting turkey-hen, clucking and gobbling in sympathetic agreement.

'*Ne*', grinned her son Manolis who had brought us over the winding stony roads from Paleochora on the coast to meet his parents, '*Kathemerinos ine etsi* – daily it is like this. Half a bottle of *tsikouthia* before midday and then a litre bottle of wine with his meal. And then he sings! *Ne*, you shall hear! And then he falls asleep and snores! *Mana mou* how he snores! They say he can be heard in Kakodiki across the ridge and they think it is thunder! *Ne!* And when he awakens he starts again!' He raised his right hand, clenched it, opened his mouth wide and pointed toward it with his extended thumb. 'Glou! Glou! Glou! Glou! Glou!' he said. '*Etsi*. Like that – glou! glou! glou! glou! glou!' He turned to his father, '*Ine sosta patera mou? It is true my father, ne?*' Andonis squinted at him with one eye closed. '*Ah scarsi*', he said, good-naturedly, 'shut up!' And draining his raki he banged both hands upon the table and rose authoritatively. '*Ella!*' he said. 'Come! Let us go and kill the pig.'

It was the first indication that we were to be treated to a divertissement, and luncheon. Obediently we followed him out of the little garden, down a rock-strewn slope to a pigsty and witnessed the quick, noiseless and expert execution, disembowelling, skinning and decapitation of a hog together with five pink piglets all unconcerned by Daddy's fate and a circle of assorted-coloured worm-eaten cats of divers ages who twitched their whiskers expectantly and waited for the viscera. One hour later the washed carcass swung from a tree in the courtyard and was jointed by Manolis, pausing only to brush away the flies, while its grinning head wrapped in eternal slumber gazed at the scene with unseeing eyes from a canvas chair by the kitchen door as its several parts were thrown into blue polythene bags and stacked in the shade.

'*Endaxi?*' enquired Andonis as he stuck his head under a stand-pipe and turned the running water pink with the sun-dried blood from his hands and arms. 'OK?' '*Endaxi!*' echoed Mandolis, rubbing the sweat from his brow with the back of his arm and wiping the knife down his trousers. 'It is finished'. '*Bravo!*' said his mother appearing with a metal tray and bearing away the choice pieces set aside. 'In one hour we shall eat, *ne?*' '*Ne*', said Andonis, towelling his dripping head with a piece of sacking and advancing toward the table, 'but first a little wine, and *mezé* . . .'

It was two o'clock by the sun when we all sat down at a groaning table in a shady room away from the flies and the afternoon heat, and overlooked by a legion of relatives past and present who stared down upon us from faded sepia photographs upon the wall. Fierce grandfathers with huge moustaches curling upward toward their brows, hooked-nosed fathers with eyes like eagles, wearing their traditional dress with pride, uncles, aunts and great-grandchildren, cousins, daughters, sisters, sons – all watched us as we attacked the feast. And how we did eat! Of pork chops and liver and freshly picked spinach; of potatoes in oil and over-cooked fish; of olives marinated in lemon juice and cheese made from a mixture of goat and sheep's milk; of red peppers and a great green salad, and an *ekatostariko* of home-made wine. And as our glasses clinked and our voices rose and the room filled with chatter and laughter, Andonis, replete, happy and redder than ever, leaned back in his chair with his arms hanging limp, threw back his head and sang the afternoon away. His voice was bass with that strange nasal quality possessed of all the Greeks and he sang with passion of the struggles of his island race; of their fight against the Turks and Germans, of peace and war and love and hate, and with every glass his voice grew louder until it seemed that the very pictures upon the walls must tremble on their hooks and come a-crashing down. It was a magnificent, moving performance.

When we left, laden with gifts – a bottle of olive oil and one of wine, a bag of olives and a single blood-red rose for Maria, kissed and pressed against her cheek by Andonis' wife, and a bunch of *vasilico* for me – Andonis was still quite sober but patently ready to disturb the valley with his snores. '*Efharistume,*' we said as we embraced and hugged,

. . . sang the afternoon away . . .

21

'*sas efharisto ya tin philoxenia sas* – thank you for your hospitality.' '*Philoxenia?*' roared Andonis, '*philoxenia? Mana mou!* It was nothing, you understand, nothing! My God! In my father's day your bellies would have been swollen with food. *Ne!* You would not have been able to stand, you understand. *Ne,* – *that* was *philoxenia!* But now?' He tilted his head back, raised his eyebrows and made a tired circular gesture with his open hand. It was, he implied, too hard and sad to explain. We embraced again. '*Sto kalo,*' he said, and rubbed his eyes. '*Ne,*' said Anatasia, '*keo Theos mazi su* – and God be with you.' It was as if we had known each other for a thousand years.

Sweating, three abreast and sardined in the cab of Manolis' fifteen-year-old springless pick-up, we waved our goodbyes until we could see them no longer through the dust clouds in our wake, and over the strident bouzoukoi music blaring from its worn-out speaker below the chipped and sun-baked plastic dashboard, shouting our thanks to him for his parents' warmth and kindness. '*Tipota!*' he bellowed back, 'don't mention it!' and braked hard, making a smell of burning rubber, to avoid a goat as we rounded a hairpin bend. 'But', he continued, as the polythene bags of pig meat on the back seat bounced skywards and a string of worry beads and a blanched icon jigged together on the fly-bespattered windscreen, 'my father was sad he did so little. *Ne, ne, ne,*' he said, drowning our protestations and taking both hands from the wheel, 'it is so. His generation feels the passing of *philoxenia* as they knew it. To them it was almost a sacred thing. He has never left Crete you understand? But he watches the television, *ne?* He sees the changes and hates them. *Mana mou!* To hear him talk you would think that the spirit of Greece is on the *necrotophia,* the cemetery! But as I tell him, *ine e zoi* – it is life.' And he crashed his gears at another bend and turned the cassette player higher.

Manolis was right: it *is* life; but change is never easy to accept, particularly with advancing years, and I could well understand his father's fears and those of many of his contemporaries who twirl their *kombouloi* and sigh when they see or hear of villages long since deserted by the young in search of material prosperity in Athens and foreign capitals, and where now only children and the old remain. 'Soon', they say, 'our villages will die or be turned into places for making films or holidays; but certainly our way of life will go.' And they shake their heads and peer darkly into their empty coffee cups like present-day Cassandras.

Maybe their gloomy prognosis will be proved correct; time alone will tell and I doubt if I shall live to know the truth; but I believe that *philoxenia* will take an unconscionable while to die in the Grecian hills and hamlets, and the more remote the area, the longer it will survive. Those are the places which call to me from across the seas and where, much though I love my motherland, my heart lies. Greece is my mistress and she will always enchant me, no matter how she ages and changes; but my love affair with her blossomed long before I set foot upon her soil. It began many years ago in an English public school.

2
Olympus Calls

'My boy,' said my mathematics master one wet May morning as he eyed me with thinly veiled malevolence over rimless half-glasses after yet another singularly unproductive lesson in elementary algebra, 'I am told that your Latin is passable; that your Greek is good, and that you have a way with words, whatever,' and here he paused to allow his eyebrows to approach his hairline, 'that may mean. But allow me to advise you', he continued acidly as they returned to their normal position, 'that the only advantage of an aptitude for the classics is that it will enable you to despise the wealth it will prevent you from earning.'

Slowly he ran the tip of his tongue from right to left across tight mean lips and smiled mirthlessly. I dug my finger-nails deep into my palms turning my knuckles white and wished him to perdition.

He was an unpleasant, small man with thin, oiled black hair, low parted and stranded economically across a balding head, and possessed of a stained fly-front to his trousers. Uncharitable boys said that he was incontinent but for my part I limited my character assassination of him by entertaining the fancy that, like one of Shakespeare's murderers, he had been born with teeth.

However, his assessment of my intellectual strengths and foibles was accurate in every particular. Mathematics in all branches of the discipline were anathema to me, and words did come readily to my lips. And he was correct in his appreciation of my love for the myths and men of ancient Greece, excluding, it must be said, those mathematical giants Euclid and Pythagoras and others of their calling. Never once, for

24

example, was I moved to emulate Archimedes and to rush naked and soap-sudded from a chipped white antiquarian bath and through the school quadrangle crying, 'Eureka! Matron! Come and see – my body weight in water's left the tub!' Nor, unlike him, did I care one jot or one iota if any person cast a shadow on my circles although I was sorry that a Roman sword had ended his deliberations in Syracuse with such indecent haste. But oh! those other heroes of that bygone age – how I was drawn to them.

In my mind's eye and aided by my classics tutor, an actor *manqué* of some forty years, a genius who made cold print leap from a page and into reality, I sailed with Jason in the *Argo* in search of the fabled Golden Fleece, charged with Achilles in the Trojan wars, flew with Perseus to the rescue of Andromeda and was at Hercules's side when he captured the Cretan Bull and brought it on his back across the sea to Argolis. These were the men who filled my boyhood dreams and helped me pass long hours away during other lessons in stuffy classrooms heavy with the smell of chalk dust and stale Stephens ink, and I minded not that the stories were untrue. Nor in those early teenage days was I distressed by the moral behaviour of some of the gods, although it did seem to me that Chronos with his sickle went a little too far with his father even though he was only doing what Mother told him; and with regard to Zeus I found most of his encounters with women, both mortals and immortals, innocent enough. As a naive and late physical developer I saw no badness in his turning himself into a cuckoo in order to be with Hera nor, for that matter, assuming the guise of a swan so that he might enjoy the company of Leda. Both seemed nice enough girls and I could well understand his wish to get to know them better, but once I had crossed the threshold of pubescence and fallen in love with my housemaster's daughter, a virtuous young woman ten years my senior, I envied him his power of metamorphosis.

I spent many a sleepless night tossing on my dormitory bed and wishing that like my hero I too could change into a shower of gold and cascade into my latter-day Danae's chamber. But until that moment when I yearned for ichor in my veins and craved for Asclepius's balm to soothe my acne, I was content to gaze through a classroom window, my head cupped in my hands, to see, not unclad elms revealing naked rookeries against grey skies, but sun-drenched Zeus standing tall upon the snow-capped peaks of Olympus and hurling thunderbolts and lightning shafts at the Titan armies or,when my conceits were less charitable, at the head of my mathematical tormentor. And in my ears, heedless of a geography master's voice droning like a superannuated bee about the products of the USA, I heard the roar of battle as with an unwearying hand the king of the heavens flung bolt after bolt at the infernal and shortly-to-be defeated Titans and filled the air with sound and fancy. I felt the earth shudder and watched vast forests burn, smelt the stench of sulphur in my nostrils and saw the mighty River Ocean boil until –

'Boy! Have we been dreaming yet again, boy?' Night's child Nemesis, black-gowned, tall and bony had arrived unheard and stood beside my desk.

'No Sir – I mean, yes – Sir – please Sir. I – I . . .' Gauntly he looked down upon me and mockingly echoed my reply.

'No Sir, yes Sir, three-bags-full Sir . . . quite so, quite so. Then pray Sir,' he inquired, bending toward me with his hands tight clasped behind his gown, 'advise me, nay enlighten all of us', – and here he raised his hands in supplication toward the ceiling, 'of the stuff of which your dreams are made.'

The class sniggered and I felt my face grow hot. Tongue tied, I wished the ground could envelop me. 'Oh come now Sir,' persisted Nemesis, inclining to me yet again; 'no reticence if you please. I insist you share with us your riches. Come, I say! Stand up and admit us to your world of dreams, your reveries, your fantasies.' He paused expectantly. 'Well?' he said; and waited.

Nervously I cleared my throat, swallowed hard and took the plunge. 'It was Greeks,' I stammered. 'I was thinking about Greeks. Greek gods, Sir . . . actually.' The class tittered again.

. . . dreaming yet again, boy? . . .

27

Slowly he straightened and drew in his breath. 'Greek . . .
gods?' he repeated, distilling and savouring each word to the
joy of my fellows, by now pregnant with expectation for the
coup de grâce, 'Greek gods?' Wordless, I nodded confirmation,
my eyes fixed upon his shoes. 'I see,' said he, and turned
away. 'Ah yes', he continued, his voice heavy with irony, and
advancing with measured tread toward the blackboard, slowly
twiddling his thumbs behind his back en route and conscious
of his audience, 'the Greeks! That splendid race who had a
word for everything. Is that not so, boy?' he inquired of the
ceiling. 'Is that not so?' He halted before his desk. Then, with
a swish of his gown he spun around to face me once again.
'Then let us all hope, boy', he snapped, 'that they will come
to your aid, for shortly you will be in need of words. Three
hundred to be precise: on the cotton pickers of Alabama; and
to be in my hands after breakfast tomorrow.'

I was not a vindictive youth but that night, long after the
dormitory lights were out, I played the eagle to his Prometheus
and relished every beakful of his liver.

Not all my masters were as out of sympathy with me as
that geographer who rejoiced in the unfortunate nickname of
Bogue, a title bestowed upon him as a result of his unpleasing
and frequent habit of picking his nose, but life at an English
public school in the mid-thirties was no easy option – particularly for romantics. Nevertheless I was indebted to that
establishment for it was within its walls that my love affair
with Greece began.

Fired and inspired by the epic magic of Homer's *Odyssey* and
Iliad and Hesiod's *Theogony*, that poem of the eighth century
BC explicitly featuring the exploits of the good, bad, brave and
randy of the Greek pantheon, together with their lineage and
order of appearance, a work which assuredly would have sent
a Longford of the period a-reaching for his pen and sal vola-
tile, I was enchanted into a world of centaurs, dryads, fauns
and naiads – a legendary epoch when Zeus reigned from the
mountain tops, Hades governed the underworld and Poseidon
ruled the seas – and thence into the later age when factual deeds

of heroism were performed and they themselves gave birth to myths. As classical scholars are still discovering, Greek facts and fables are often difficult to disentangle; but it was in my penultimate term of school, in the late autumn of 1940, that I was made aware of contemporary and unembellished Greek tragedy and bravery.

On the 28th of October, a month or so after the Battle of Britain had been fought and won, when the cat's-cradles of vapour trails from Heinkels, Hurricanes and Dorniers high up in English skies had all but vanished, the Italian minister in Athens – basking in the victories of the seemingly unassailable German armies which had blitzkrieged their ways through Europe, and when the Axis powers reigned supreme – presented an ultimatum to the Greeks: 'Surrender to Albania, and so to us, your lands of Epirus, or else!' And with one voice the nation answered '*Oche!*' 'No!' Three weeks later they chased the organ grinders from Grecian soil and back into Albania and ignominy. It was a day when, as I was to be told in later years by a peasant woman, emotional and crow-black in her widow's weeds in a village in south-west Crete, 'even the stones of Greece rose up to fight the invader.' And her eyes glistened and she dabbed them with the hem of her headscarf. '*Ne*,' she said, 'it was *philotimo* which urged our people on and drove those barbarians back! *Philotimo*! Pride! *Katalavis Yanni mou* – you understand, my Yanni?' And I nodded and said that I did. And it was that same pride which centuries before had freed them from the Turkish yoke that, in the May of 1941 when Crete had been overwhelmed by the airborne might of the *Luftwaffe* and the Allied troops had evacuated the island, sent young men and boys deep into the Cretan hills to continue the fight against the Germans. Their land was occupied, but unconquered. Twelve-year-olds, teenagers and the middle-aged, descendants of the Homeric heroes of Ancient Greece, their valour undiminished by the sands of time, all fought like lions against the aggressor; and as a sixth-former on the brink of joining in the war my heart went out to them.

I remember those dark days so well; for the grim headlines

in the daily papers; for the tears which a Greek doctor friend of my father shed when Athens fell; and for the reading of the names of the first casualties suffered by the school – four boys of the Upper Sixth, a year senior to me, who had fallen in the Battle of Crete. One day, I thought, I would visit their graves near Souda Bay and Maleme on the north-west coast and over forty summers later I did so; but that was not my first excursion to my land of dreams.

In the summer of 1968 I boarded the SS *Uganda*, of Falklands fame but now, alas, reduced to razor blades, as the guest speaker to a minority of independent cabin passengers and a consortium of preparatory schools who had booked the vessel for the purpose of broadening the horizons of their privileged charges and instructing them in the ways of the ancient races of the Mediterranean. It was a remarkable voyage made poignant for me by a resistible woman of indeterminate years with a penchant for Etruscan urns in particular and men in general regardless of their ethnic origins, and a headmaster with an impeccable lineage but dubious scholastic abilities.

Excluding meal and lecture periods, the former – aptly named Diana – pursued me from sunrise to sunset between the boat deck and scuppers while the latter, whom fate had ordained to be my immediate table companion, complained each breakfast time that the menu was innocent of Rose's Lime Marmalade. Rose's Lime Marmalade, he rumbled to the rest of the table as silently they spread their toast with Gentleman's Relish or coarse-peeled orange Oxford, had always been provided for him on previous cruises. It was, he advanced, well-known by British India, not to mention the Peninsular and Orient Line, that the inclusion of Rose's Lime Marmalade was a prerequisite of his and, furthermore, as a close friend of the head of the company he would complain to that worthy about this oversight. Unbelievably, he acquired a jar of his favourite preserve at Izmir and consequently remained cloyed and content until it ran out half-way across the Sea of Marmara. Meanwhile Diana the Huntress, large and formidable with undisciplined bosoms swinging from

port to starboard at waistline level, stalked through the ship
in search of quarry.

Red-haired, loud-voiced and patently sex-starved, she was
an inexhaustable mine of information – a veritable font of
knowledge. Her interests were catholic. She pronounced on
everything and everybody. She gave us a potted history of
Stromboli as we passed the quietly smoking volcano in the
distance, treated us to a résumé of the film of the same name
starring the late Ingrid Bergman and then moralised on the
life-style of that lady. She enlightened us as to why dolphins
leapt from the sea, made us privy to the sex life of a swallow-
tailed butterfly as it fluttered on tired wings and came to rest
on a lifeboat, and held a seminar over the corpse of a flying
fish which crash-landed upon the poop. Nor did she draw
breath when we reached our first port of call after leaving
Naples, Mykonos, that expensive, garish, tourist-saturated
island in the Cyclades where legend has it the defeated Titans
lie buried but which is now a haven for lesbians, homo- and
heterosexual perverts or, as a Greek friend of mine described
it more succinctly, 'a *poushtie paradiso*'.

She knew the island's size and population, the number of
dovecots, windmills and chapels ('360 you know but they're
a Godless lot, vice and the like, that's what they're into, oh
dear me, yes.') and why all the buildings were painted with
whitewash. 'Hygiene,' she boomed; 'it keeps down the bugs,'
and then listed the several species.

She also knew the sea and air temperatures and the
strength of the wind, the fierce *meltemi* from the north which
whipped the waves around and under the overladen, plunging
and tossing caique as it took us to the neighbouring islet of
Delos, and she continued unabated as it docked and spilled
us upon the barren, sandstone rocky shores like an army of
culture-seeking ants to scatter among the ruins and artefacts
of Apollo's birthplace and the sanctuary of his mother, Leto.
Providentially, somewhere in that vast outdoor museum, I
gave her the slip and climbed alone to the top of Mount
Kynthos, the island's highest point and from that advantage

looked down upon the remains of the once prospering community of 8 BC and others long before that date.

Three hundred and fifty feet below me stretched the last vestiges of an avenue of proud marble lions who, with mouths agape, guarded the way to Leto's shrine, and nearer lay the remnants of the villas of the well-to-do, houses with richly patterned mosaic floors of dolphins, tridents, masks and gods from which the dwellings took their names. I saw my shipboard companions sitting on the relics of a horse-shoe amphitheatre, four tiers of which had been preserved, standing before the most sacred altar site of Delos the Keraton where Theseus made his sacrifices, or wandering among the *stoas* and *agora* of the city's trading quarters, and their chatter reached me on the wind. But other sounds were in my ears.

I heard Delian voices of long ago: of Romans, Greeks and men from Asia Minor, all drawn to the island by the lodestone of commerce; merchants, bankers and slave-traders, arguing, bargaining over prices, jostling each other in the narrow streets and clamouring in the market-places. And I heard the cries of street vendors and the bleating of goats and the notes of the *lyra* and the chanting of priests . . . Those were the noises the breeze brought to me and I listened enrapt as it blew back the pages of time.

For a long while I stood there, my hands deep in my trouser pockets, blissfully content with my flights of fancy and the panorama below me. At last, I mused, I was alone; and in Greece. Then, knocking my pipe out on the palm of my hand and grinding the dottle into the dust, I turned my back on the scorched brown earth and looked out toward the dark blue of the Mirtoan Sea. There in the distance lay the scattered chips of other Cycladean islands: Naxos, Paros, Siphnos and Seriphos, 'the wheeling ones' as the Ancients called them for they surrounded the hub of sacred Delos, and I stared at them in reverie, lost in thought and dreaming of the days when I might visit them. And then it happened.

Panting and purple from her climb, the dreadful Diana re-entered my life. 'Hallo!' she bellowed against the wind.

'It's only little me. Spiffing view don't you think?' she yelled, and told me the names of the islands.

As I was to discover to my cost, there is a Diana in every cruise ship. Seven years later I met her *Doppelgänger* aboard the same craft. On that occasion she was dressed in tweeds and spoke in the incisive accents of Edinburgh; but I have immortalised her in another book. However, accomplished though that Jenner-clad counterpart was, she held not a candle to the ineffable Diana who ruined that day for me in Delos. Thirty-six hours later she repeated the experience – in Ephesus. But the danger-cones were hoisted shortly after breakfast in Izmir, to where we had sailed from Mykonos laden with overpriced sponges and undersized loofahs.

'Can't wait to get to Ephesus,' she boomed as a number of us sat together in the saloon awaiting our call for transport to the site. 'I really just can't *wait*.' 'Really?' said the hitherto marmalade-deprived headmaster, fresh from his recent shopping spree ashore as he addressed himself to his post-breakfast Horse's Neck, 'Why?' 'Why?' exclaimed Diana incredulously, her green eyes bulging beneath short ginger lashes. 'Why? *Because*', said she, 'that's where my temple is, that's why! My temple don't you know – the Temple of Diana! Diana of the Ephesians and all that! Ha! Ha! Ha! Ha! Ha!' And she brayed loudly and dug him in the ribs with her elbow as he sipped at his restorative. Glassily he watched the mixture of brandy and ginger ale soak into his shirt, and was not amused. Nor were those nearest to her in the coach which bore us to that ruined city.

It was a long, hot and dusty journey to Ephesus, made even more tedious by her delivery of a largely inaccurate Reader's Digest account of Saint Paul's missionary work within its precincts, imparted to us in competition with that of the driver's mate which crackled to us through an errant hand-held microphone. After five minutes he gave up the unequal task and took his revenge by turning off the air-conditioning. She told us that the bee was the symbol of Ephesus, and why; gave us a blow-by-blow summation of the silversmiths' riot and how it started; advised us that Saint Paul had piles and was not only a troublemaker but a misogynist to boot, and held forth largely about the power of Diana. But she saved her party piece until the afternoon.

In company with an Anglican ex-Eton Chaplain, a splendid Christian gentleman seldom seen without a glass in his hand and his free arm around a woman's waist, I sat in the theatre of Ephesus and from one of the stone tiers set high above looked down upon the huge semi-circle below us and beyond to where across the marsh a road had once led to the harbour of Ephesus. We sat there quietly smoking our pipes and both conscious that in that great arena, once capable of seating twenty-four thousand people, maybe in AD 55, a silversmith named Demetrius had incited his fellow workers to revolt against the preaching of Saint Paul. And as in Delos the air was filled with clamour. And as in Delos, the dream was shattered.

Into the stone-strewn U below came the ubiquitous Diana. With what and where she had refreshed herself since leaving the coach is academic but clearly she was feeling little pain. 'My God,' murmured His Reverence as she staggered from stage right to stage left and thence to centre, 'she's pissed!'

Below, and oblivious of her spellbound audience, Diana described two uncertain circles as if enacting a slow-motion solo of ring-a-ring-a-roses, caught her foot on a stunted twig, and then sat down abruptly. 'Shit!' she said, proving the excellence of the acoustic quality of the site, and momentarily stared at the ground. Then, levering herself to an upright position and retaining the posture with difficulty, with feet astride and arms outstretched, she threw back her head and bellowed thickly to the surrounding hills: 'Great – ish – Diana! Great – ish – Diana – of the, of the – Eph, Eph, Ephesians!' And whirling her open handbag around her head, she scattered its contents in all directions, and involuntarily sat down again.

'Dear Lord!' said my companion removing his pipe as we gazed in mutual disbelief at the macabre spectacle before us. 'I can't help thinking that if the good Saint Paul was with us today he'd have been hard-pushed to write about charity to anyone, let alone the Corinthians; but I think we ought to help her. After all,' he said, 'we pass through this life but once and so on, which', he added, pointing with his pipe stem to the stricken Diana now on all fours and groping for her possessions, 'is probably just as well.'

I do not know what happened to Diana, but in retrospect I felt sorry for her. She was one of that sad, lonely, roving, moneyed band of women who board the cruise ships and sail the seas in search of companionship and love, and seldom find either. As for my dog-collared friend of yesteryear he has long since departed for celestial pastures where no doubt he is attempting to seduce the angels, but I did meet up with him on another cruise in 1975, and became devoted to him. It was then we visited Corinth.

Together we watched the more elderly of our company make bee-lines for a sign spelled TOOLETE written in crazed red capitals on the wall of a roadside tourist *cafeneon* in front of which we had debussed after the drive from Piraeus, declined the glass of ouzo included in the price of the excursion, and disengaged ourselves from the coachloads. Ten minutes later and from a tan-coloured mountain we looked down on the site of the Corinth of Saint Paul – a young, brash, commercial city packed with Romans, Greeks and Jews, all attracted to a metropolis with no tradition save that of making money and possessed of every conceivable vice under the Grecian sun; but until that day I was ignorant of the word 'corinthianise' which had been coined to describe an evil life. That, I learned from my companion.

He was a fine Pauline scholar and he taught me much that cloudless morning, for it was he who turned Saint Paul into flesh and blood and made him come alive for me. It was thanks to him that I saw Paul through fresh eyes, not as the saint, but as the uncanonised, middle-aged, hook-nosed, hairy little Jewish widower with a twitch who, with Athenian mocking still in his ears and the marks of Philippian rods still on his back, limped bow-legged into that moral sewer and stayed for eighteen months, preaching the gospel of Christ. And I listened intently as he unfolded the story.

'My God,' I said, not as a blasphemy but as a prayer, 'I must say he had guts, didn't he?' 'Oh yes,' said my friend, 'he was tough all right. He must have been to have kept going in that cesspool, and after. And don't forget,' he added, 'he was dammed ill at the time which wasn't really surprising, poor sod.' And he laughed quietly and rummaged in his pockets for his pipe and pouch. 'After all', he said, 'he'd been through the mill when you think about it. I mean,' he continued, as he filled the bowl, 'I doubt if either of us could take, what was it? one stoning, three beatings by the Romans, five by the Jews – and most of those on an empty stomach – and still come up smiling. *And* he was shipwrecked three times remember; *and* chucked into jug more than once. Oh yes, he had guts – plenty of 'em. In fact,' he went on, 'now I come to consider it he'd have made a splendid scrum-half, if he could have seen the ball, that is. He had dreadful opthalmia you know.'

As I have hinted and as old Etonians would testify, my friend was no ordinary dyed-in-the-wool cleric. He paused to light his pipe with a Swan Vesta. 'But you know,' he continued, applying the flame and tamping the tobacco down between puffs with his forefinger, 'what really makes me admire the chap isn't so much his physical courage, but his moral strength; his belief in his faith, his ability to bounce back, never to give in to adversity. I tell you, so far as I'm concerned, he was one of the greatest of the Apostles.'

He struck another match and reignited the stubborn tobacco. 'For instance,' he postulated, repeating the kindling, 'just suppose, for the sake of argument, that you spent a year and a half working all the hours that God gave you, devoting yourself, and against an active opposition, to building up an institution or society, or business if you like, in which you believed more deeply than anything else, and despite all the odds, *succeeded*. You'd be pretty chuffed, wouldn't you?' I nodded. 'Yes,' I said, 'I would.' 'But then suppose,' he advanced, pursuing the analogy, 'that within a very short while

of leaving this flourishing establishment, you heard that it had
gone to pot; that everything for which you'd worked had been
in vain – what would your reaction be then?'

I shrugged my shoulders. 'Hard to say,' I admitted. 'Dis-
illusionment perhaps? Despair? Anger?' 'Exactly!' he said,
and stabbed the air with his pipe. 'And mine. But you know
that's what happened here after Paul left,' and in under three
years too. The whole community went to the dogs. Oh yes,'
he said, 'infighting among the priests, sodomy, rape, incest,
the lot. And *that*', he emphasised, 'was the news which Paul
had to stomach when it reached him in Ephesus; and he was
having a pretty thin time of it there, don't forget.' He paused
and began to chuckle. 'Lord!' he said, reflectively, 'Ephesus!
Remember Diana?' 'I do,' I said, 'as if it were yesterday,' and
we laughed. 'But to get back to Paul,' he resumed, 'and he
must have been shattered when he learned all that, *his* reaction
was the opposite of what our would have been. You see, for a
start he didn't say "Oh God! – to hell with it!" or words to that
effect and pronounce himself a failure; nor did he fly into a rage
and write a stinker to the Corinthians denouncing them. No, he
didn't do that. Instead, he sat down and dictated – he couldn't
see very well at the time you understand – what I think is one
of the most moving passages of all time.' He glanced towards
me, quizzingly. 'Remember it?' I nodded. 'Um,' I said, 'the
one about faith, hope and charity.' 'That's it,' he said. 'And
the greatest of these is charity, or, as the New English Bible
has it, "love".'

For half a minute or so he remained silent, quietly pulling
at his pipe. Then: 'What a pity,' he said, 'that most of the world
has forgotten that.' And he slapped me on the shoulder, and
smiled. 'Here endeth the first lesson,' he said . . .

I went to bed early that night. And in the quiet of
my cabin with the sound of the sea slip-slopping against
the hull as we steamed toward Alexandria, I read the whole
of Saint Paul's first epistle to the Corinthians; and before I
went to sleep I reread his thirteenth chapter. '... Though
I speak with the tongues of men and of angels, and have

not charity, I am become as sounding brass, or a tinkling cymbal . . .'

That was the last *en masse* excursion I made to Greece, and looking back I marvel that I emerged unscathed if noticeably greyer. The life of a guest 'celebrity' aboard is not a bed of roses – the Dianas of this world make sure of that – but I was not ungrateful to the British India Steamship Company who allowed me to work my passage. Under their auspices I met people like my reverend friend of blessed memory who enriched my life at Ephesus and Corinth, and Maria to whom I lost my heart under a Cycladean sky and who was destined to be with me on many of my journeys to the islands. But that mode of travel did not enable me to reach the heart of Greece and touch its hub. And so it was that in 1976 I embarked upon a private odyssey which has continued ever since.

3
Ine e Zoi – That's Life

Knowing no modern Greek, the popular *demotiki*, so very different from the tongue of Homer but no more easy to learn, I went twice in 1976 to Andros in the Cyclades, that beautiful island an hour's sail from Raffina on the mainland, and saw her freshly dressed for spring in a carpet of flowers, and more drably clad in autumn. In following years I went to Kos, and to other islands in the Dodecanese; to Kalymnos where the sponge fishers live; to isolated, volcanic Nisyros where the air is heavy with the smell of sulphur; to Karpathos and Simi; and to untouched villages in Rhodes. And so the months passed, and my knowledge of the Greek people grew.

Daily I sat in small *tavernas* and dingy ill-lit *cafeneons*, understanding little but absorbing the ambience and watching the old, cloth-capped unshaven men whiling their hours away over coffee cups which never seemed to empty and ouzo glasses which never ran dry. Slowly they sipped, lethargically split roasted pumpkin seeds between their teeth and talked in bellows across retsina-stained plastic table-tops or, in silence, trickled the beads of their *kombouloi* through gnarled fingers, watching the world go by through the smoke of interminable cigarettes while others read the news of the day or played backgammon sending the dice clattering across the board with a cry of 'Oopah!' and a clap of the hands. And always, somewhere in the background, the non-stop sound of canned bouzoukoi music.

That was the atmosphere in which I learned my Greek, among the Yannis and Yiorgos, Manolises and Nikoses, the peasant farmers and fishermen of the islands. Those were my tutors. Simple, honest, ungrammatical, rough-spoken and

39

often edentate men with huge hands and even bigger hearts who banged on the tables when I got a word right and never mocked me when I failed. '*Bravo Yanni!*' they would shout, and reward me with retsina.

They were happy tutorials. I learned how to say good morning, good evening, goodnight and good gracious, and frequently used the salutations and partings in the wrong order. Even more repeatedly I gave the wrong inflection or, by the substitution of a single letter, mouthed the wrong word. Hourly I made a fool of myself but my *faux pas* were accepted sympathetically by the Greeks. Doubtless they laughed behind my back, but never to my face. "Ah," they said, one to another in my presence but as though I was absent from the scene, 'he tries, he tries – *Mana mou* how he tries!' And thus encouraged I blundered on, leaving an ever-lengthening trail of gaffes behind me.

Unwittingly, I expressed a penchant for cicadas for supper instead of *tzatziki*, that delicious pot-pourri of cucumber, yoghurt, garlic and oil served with other *mezé* before the main dish, and on one never-to-be-forgotten occasion when supping with friends and intending to ask for bread, I boldy announced that I had an erection. As a conversation-stopper it was a huge success and one which I have yet to equal. Maria, who was with me at the time, was patted on the back and told how lucky she was; and as her cheeks reddened and she bowed her head, I was congratulated in similar style. 'Truly,' I was advised, 'to do that *and* to eat and drink at the same time is *katapliktiko* – fantastic!' But little by little I began to speak appalling Greek extremely well, and I have never looked back.

That incident happened some years ago in a Rhodian village called Gennadi with which we fell in love, both with the place and with its inhabitants; but they have never allowed us to forget the moment. 'Ah,' they said when we revisited the village in 1986, 'do you remember that September night in Savas's *cafeneon* when, ha! Ha! Ha! . . .' and they clenched their fists, bent their forearms and gestured upward. 'Po! Po!

Po!' they said, and had hysterics. But for us that last visit was both sweet and sour.

Two years previously, in a magazine which catered for the Grecophile and extolling the virtues of the village, I wrote 'Gennadi is a safe haven for the true lovers of Greece. The big operators will never move in as they have elsewhere for there is little to attract them . . .'

I was wrong. As we drove slowly toward Gennadi to be reunited with our friends after a two-year absence, a quarter of a mile from the old, long, tree-lined avenue which leads to the village square where the bus from Rhodes ends its journey, we saw a new, freshly bulldozed road climbing to the heights above the village. It led to a nearly completed concrete complex of hotels and three-storeyed tourist apartment blocks. The big operators *had* moved in. We stopped, staring at the monstrous eyesore in silence; and then at each other. 'Oh no!' said Maria. 'Oh yes', said I, and drove on into the village, and past another holiday block.

It took only a few hours for us to see the full extent of the developments in what once had been a sleepy backwater of less than three hundred souls. Pensions and small hotels in varying stages of construction stood on the open spaces flanking the road to the sea, and in the winding narrow streets in the hub of the village old houses, the properties of returning ex-patriots, had been demolished and new dwellings erected on their sites. Most of them had 'Rooms to Rent' signs in their windows. Of the two old *cafeneons*, only one remained as such. The other had been converted and flashed a horrid neon legend saying 'Cocktails' above its door, while inside international pop music blared and a strange young man with a waiter's napkin moved between new pine tables and varnished tree-stumps serving as stools. The lights were low and the prices high and we hurried by, past yet more flashing signs from an 'Ice Cream Parlour' with a video game, to fat old Savas's place to sit on rickety rush-seated chairs and to feel at home in the honest grime and among the less sophisticated.

They at least had not changed: Pandelis the drunk who

41

worked as a stoker on the night shifts at the nearby brick factory and who wore a permanent mask of soot; Karayanni the fisherman who never caught anything; Manolis the deaf mute with a new hearing-aid which gave him access to a hitherto hidden world of sound; Lukas the house-painter in a whitewash-splattered shirt; Dimitri the elderly grocer from across the street together with his little granddaughter whose birth we remembered; bald Savas himself, bigger bellied than ever and still wearing the same spectacles with the thick cracked lenses that he had when we first met him in 1981; and Mary his wife with her arthritic hips, and their bad-tempered cat, Admetus. All were there, and all embraced us with gusto and noise. Pandelis enveloped us in an aura of stale sweat and ceramic dust, Admetus the evil ginger tom, upset and excited by the hullabaloo, sprang into the air and sank its teeth into Savas's thigh, and everyone bought us ouzo. *'Kalso orisate!'* they cried as the glasses clinked, 'welcome! Welcome back!' *'Kalos sas vrikame!'* we yelled in reply. 'But hasn't Gennadi altered?' 'Ah,' they said, 'it has changed indeed,' and one by one, excluding Pandelis who was incapable of coherent speech but including Manolis who used sign language, all expressed an opinion about the new complex at the top of the hill.

'Po! Po! Po!' said Karayanni. 'Two hundred beds in the hotel alone – they will swamp us with their numbers! They will', he advanced, 'bring havoc to the village, these *aspros* – these white ones!' And he banged his glass upon the table and gestured for more ouzo.

'Ne,' agreed Mary as she rose painfully in search of the bottle, 'they will, they will. And the *askimos*, the rough young ones with their coloured hair from England and other countries, they will get drunk and fight as I have heard they do in Lindos and Faliraki. *Ne,'* she said as she filled the glasses, 'they will bring us many problems and much noise.' 'Maybe,' wheezed Savas stroking the now recovered Admetus on his lap, 'but they will also bring more trade you understand.' And he smiled and rubbed his thumb and forefinger together. *'Poli lepta,'* he said, 'plenty money.'

'*Ne*,' endorsed Lukas scratching himself under his left armpit, '*poli*! And more work for me on the new houses which will be built as the village grows. Oh yes, much more money.' 'Ah!' shouted Karayanni pulling Lukas's hat down over his face, '*capitolisti*, that is what you are! Just like the Thatcher woman, you understand. Po! Po! Po! What would Papandreou say if he had heard such things!' And he gave Lukas a playful smack on the head. 'That is so,' grinned Lukas as he came up for air. 'But will you turn up *your* nose at the tourists who will pay you for taking them out in your boat – will you?' '*Ne! Ne!*' exclaimed old Dimitri from the corner. 'Will you? I tell you my friend, for my opinion you will have more of them in your nets than fish! And if that does not happen then I will put a nail through my nose. *Etsi,*' he said, 'like this', and mimicked the action with his finger. 'But,' he continued, as the laughter died down and addressing the two of us, 'there is one other matter my children.' And he looked toward his granddaughter who was playing with two other little girls in front of the *cafeneon*.

'Katrina,' he called, '*ella agape mou* – come my love', and the child skipped toward him together with her companions. 'You see,' he said, kissing her and settling her upon his knee and putting his arm around the other children, 'at my age I too dislike change and hustle and bustle. I was born here. I love the village, you understand. But one must think of this generation and what the future holds for them. If Gennadi does not prosper then they will be forced to search for work in other countries as many of my generation did, when the village became a ghost town, and once again Gennadi will die. But if it thrives then they will stay. So will their children and grandchildren, and Gennadi will be alive, long after they are dead. Is it not like that?' he asked of the others who had listened with deference to their eldest statesman. '*Ne,*' they murmured, 'it is like that.'

He looked at us again. '*Katalavis* Yanni? *Katalavis* Maria?' '*Ne,*' we said, '*katalavenome* – we understand.' '*Endaxi,*' he said, easing Katrina from his knee and slowly standing up,

43

'but now it is time for old men to go to bed, and', he added, taking Katrina by the hand, 'little people too. *Kali nichta,*' he said, and embraced us once more. 'Enjoy your stay with us, and please, do not be saddened by the changes. It is, after all, life. *Ne?*' '*Ne,*' we said, '*ine e zoi* – it is life.'

Dimitri was right – in all respects. It was life; and wherever we went in the village during the following days, a similar story unfolded. 'My oath,' twanged an expatriate Gennadian in Australian Greek, one of the many who had emigrated from the village in the late forties and who by hard work and thrift had made his fortune running a pizza house in Adelaide and returned to retire in Gennadi, 'when I left here in '48 the place was a bloody dump, mate.' 'Yeah,' said his friend who had laboured in a Detroit car factory and spoke with the accent of that district through the stump of a chewed cigar, 'genuine Crumbsville, bud. But now it's comin' on OK I guess. Yes sir! In two years' time you won't know the place.' 'Too right you won't', agreed the New Antipodean, lighting a cigarette with a solid gold Dunhill lighter, 'Apostolis here's rebuilt his old Dad's house and let it, I've done up me uncle's place near the Square, and that', he said, 'will bring in a pile from the Krauts and Poms, oh my word it will – and we'll all sit on our arses drinking beer! And why not?' he added rhetorically and with a tinge of belligerence. 'It's our land we've come back to – yeah, too right it is! And,' he concluded, nodding toward a Cadillac parked on a nearby brick-strewn building-site, 'we've done it in style, mate.' 'Yeah,' said his friend, biting the end off a fresh cigar, 'we sure have. Have a good day folks, have a good day.'

As I said to Maria as we walked past the gleaming evidence of their deserved material prosperity, digesting this latest intelligence, there is nothing quite as Australian as a Greek Australian. But, as I remarked to her, I found them easier to understand when they spoke in Greek.

The day before we were due to leave for England, and sheltered from the midday sun by a canopy of vines, we sat in the courtyard of a tiny house in the heart of the village.

It was very basic but we had looked upon it as a home from home from the first time we had visited Gennadi. And as we sipped our ouzo, from their house three yards across the street came Lukas the decorator, his club-footed wife Poppi, a tiny tot named Soulla and two cats. '*Yasu* Yanni! *Yasu* Maria!' they called out as they swung open the rusty iron gate. '*Pos pais pethia* – how goes it, children?' '*Kala,*' we said, '*poli kala* – very good,' and watched them place a saucer of green olives, a plate of black figs, another of home-made cheese, and a hunk of bread upon the table. '*Kali oreksi!*' said little Soulla – our niece by courtesy at whose birthday party the day before we had clapped as she blew out four candles – and kissed us on our cheeks. '*Ne,*' chimed Poppi and Lukas in concert, 'good appetite! But bring back the plates when you've finished.' And shooing the cats before them they departed for their own meal.

For a while we sat there, picking at the offering and watching two house sparrows feeding their unseen young in a nest hidden in a hole near the top of Poppi's flat-topped roof, wondering if they were the same pair which had occupied that site when we had first slept in the house five years before, and, aware that our present time was running out, we fell to reminiscing. The overhead covering of vine leaves was sparser than we remembered; and chickens clucked and roosted in a shed adjoining our bedroom; and little Soulla was only a bulge in her mother's tummy. Five months later in 1982 we waved goodbye to the whole family as they crammed into a dilapidated van bound for the hospital in Rhodes while those remaining in the village crossed themselves and prayed aloud that the jolting would not induce a premature birth. And we recalled too the rejoicing when mother and child returned well and intact; when every village woman and little girl trooped past our gate in a never-ending stream to view and kiss the new-born babe, and Papa Nikolas the priest dropped in to bless it, and choked them all with incense.

So the memories came flooding back, some happy, others sad, but all about people: of births and wakes and funerals and deaths, when red rose petals were strewn along the paths

. . . choked them all with incense . . .

en route to the houses of the bereaved; of our first service in the village church when Papa Nikolas, then free of cataract, had offered us his hand to kiss, and blessed us and made us welcome; of evening strolls through the village streets to greet and be greeted by old and young; and of a day we sailed with Karayanni when Maria hooked an iridescent rosetta fish and was moved to tears as it gasped and died upon the deck, and its colours of bright orange and electric blue quickly faded in the sun. But Karayanni had said that that was life and that it was the very best to eat, better even than *barbounia*. And leaving the tiller to care for itself, he had given her a great bear-hug and told her how clever she was, and within an hour of our return to land had reported her expertise to the whole of the village. And as one man they had applauded her success.

Such were our nostalgic wanderings and we basked in the warmth of these reminders of the past. But most poignant of all our recollections was the affection and kindness which the people of Gennadi had given us. Selfishly we resented the present changes in the village and were fearful of the plans for its future development. Gennadi, we agreed, would no longer be the comfortable, compact community of yesteryear which had taken us to its heart from the very start; and we kept a sad silence for some moments.

It was Maria who broke the quietude. 'Do you think', said she, finishing her ouzo and watching a fresh libation turn to milk as I added water to the spirit, 'that we'll ever come back?' I laughed. 'You've read my thoughts,' I said, 'but yes I do', and I nodded in the direction of Lukas's house. 'Just to see them again,' I said, 'just to keep in touch.' And I filled my own glass and raised it. 'But come what may,' I said, 'I'll always think of Gennadi as it was when we first found it way back in '81. Here's to its ghost – *yasas!*'

4

The Isle of Prometheus

Excluding our discovery of Gennadi, 1981 was a vintage year for us in our exploration of the Aegean.

Mutually conscious that, despite the miracles of modern medicine, neither of us would live long enough to visit and enjoy fully all the islands in the Dodecanese, we accepted with alacrity the offer from a friend, one Colin Murison Small – a Renaissance man with a penchant for pink shirts with attached white collars, and exquisitely manicured hands – to spend two weeks in the early October of that year cruising in a craft aptly named *Small World*, together with twenty-two other Britons. 'Agreed,' said he over luncheon, appreciatively sipping the remainder of his Margaux as he listed the itinerary of our ports of call. 'You'll only stay a matter of hours in each place, but at least you'll get a sight of them. And besides that,' he smiled, dabbing his mouth with his napkin, 'your companions may cause you some amusement. And', he added, 'vice versa.'

Like ourselves, our chum is a believer that we, the British, are a funny crowd both ashore and afloat, but are blessed with the ability to laugh at ourselves. He is also a most open-handed person. Prior to our seaborne expedition, for the last few days of September, he allowed us the use of a villa on the island of Simi. Colin Murison Small is much enamoured of Simi and its people. So, too, was Homer.

'Nereus', wrote that poet, describing the king of Simi in the *Iliad*, 'is after the flawless Achilles, the handsomest man among the Danaans who descended on Troy,' but of the islands itself, which he spelt 'Syme', he offered no description. Conversely, more modern travel books using the spelling 'Simi' and more stilted prose, tell the reader that the island is rocky, mountainous, has fertile valleys and is picturesque; that it is twenty-two square miles in area, and has an indigenous population of two and a half thousand friendly natives. However, I have heard shorter appreciations.

'Simi', said Yiorgo Zagorianos, our one-eyed Greek friend of many years' standing who, with his Swedish wife Anna-Marie and innumerable stray cats, keeps a pension in Rhodes town and with whom we were staying prior to embarking for the island, 'is one long *taverna*.' '*Ya, ya*,' echoed Anna-Marie who was nursing a prematurely-born kitten and nourishing it with milk dispensed from an especially purchased doll's feeding bottle, 'so, so many of these places you might say. *Ya, ya* – all the way around the harbour. And oh my dears! The fooder! Ummm!' And she raised her eyes toward the ceiling, pursed her lips, and blew it a kiss. Anna-Marie like most of her compatriots was no mean trencherwoman and, like most Swedish ladies addicted to the pleasures of the table, she had lost her figure but retained her accent.

'O Lord!' I said, catching Maria's eye and wondering if we had been ill-advised to embrace the generosity of our friend and to stay upon the island, 'it sounds like another Mykonos.' Zagorianos laughed. 'Oh no,' he said, 'no, no, no – nothing like that,' and rose to mix himself a drink at his well-stocked bar in the corner of the room. 'For one thing,' he continued, squirting soda water into a mixture of Campari and gin, 'it hasn't any *poushties*. At least,' he qualified decorating his tipple with a maraschino-flavoured cherry, 'no more than the usual quota for these days.' Yiorgo Zagorianos, it should be explained, was born in Khartoum, speaks impeccable idiomatic English, albeit with Greek tonality, and is a cynic.

'But,' I persisted, 'from what you've said, it must be tourist-orientated.' '*Ya, ya*,' said Anna-Marie plucking the kitten's tiny claws from her right bosom and plugging in the bottle once again, 'sure, sure, the touristi-are-there, in plenty numbers, *ya*? But, she proceeded, maintaining the rhythm of her native tongue and wincing as the now ecstatic kitten reneedled its way to her flesh, 'they *keaupor.*' Maria looked puzzled. Yiorgo enlightened her. 'Cope', he said, 'they manage. In a word,' he enlarged, taking her glass and refilling it, 'uniquely they've absorbed the tourists and yet preserved their own private way of life. At any rate,' he said, returning the goblet to her, 'in the upper town they have. You see,' he continued, resuming his seat and selecting a handful of nuts from an onyx bowl beside him, 'there are two towns. The lower one at sea level, which I think was built in the nineteenth century, and the *upper* which, as you'll discover my dear Yanni,' and here he winked at Maria with his one good eye, 'is five hundred very steep steps above it.'

'*Ya, ya,*' confirmed Anna-Maria, still in the role of foster mother, 'so so-steep-the-stepping-oh-my-God! But perhaps in England,' she inquired of me, 'you do the yogging, ya?' I shook my head. 'No,' I said, 'I don't yog – er jog – at all.' 'Never mind,' said Yiorgo, 'just think of the Greek proverb my friend: "to enjoy the spiritual life to the full one must suffer physically." ' He chewed reflectively upon an almond. 'I can't remember who said it,' he admitted, 'but he must have been a Stoic. Or,' he added, 'a masochist.' And he laughed unkindly and threw a nut at me. 'But seriously,' he said, 'I'm sure you'll like Simi. Once the day-trippers have left it's very peaceful there and they only stay for an hour or two. You'll sail with them in the morning. Which reminds me,' he concluded, 'don't worry about the fares – the captain's an old friend of mine,' and he winked again. '*Philoxenia!*' he grinned. 'And now Yanni *mou*, have another drink.'

The following morning we bade adieu to Anna-Marie who was already employed on the early-morning kitten shift, and accompanied by Yiorgo in a taxi with whose driver he was on intimate terms (a happy relationship which occasioned a forty per cent reduction of the fare), we arrived at Mandraki harbour. There we were introduced to the captain who assured us that any friend of Yiorgo's was a friend of his, or words to that effect, and we listened to him instructing the first mate that our every wish *en voyage* should be granted; then, in company with a motley crowd of tourists drawn from every stratum of English society, boarded the vessel scheduled to leave at half past eight of the clock on the Wednesday of September the 23rd. True to the best tradition of Greek time-keeping it slipped its moorings at nine fifteen.

It was an interesting crossing made poignant by our fellow travellers. We eavesdropped unashamedly. We learned that calamine lotion was effective against prickly heat but that it came off on the sheets; that moussaka was only tarted up shepherd's pie and shouldn't be given house room; that aubergines were a powerful diuretic; and that young Greek males have lovely tight bums – this last intelligence gleaned from a Middlesborough woman who advised all within earshot that the older you were the younger you wanted them and that she was sure we knew what she meant. But the *pièce de résistance* came from three Americans.

They were a bizarre trio. All in their late fifties and filled to overflowing with that abundance of bonhommie with which most of our transatlantic cousins seem to be endowed, and determined to show the world in general that they were regular American guys and as such should be loved universally, they conversed in bellows, shouted 'Yahoo! Yippee!' and 'Hi!' to neighbouring ships as we left the harbour, and then sat down to a boisterous row with their backs to the stern.

'Gee,' said one whose name was Marvin, 'isn't this just great, fellers?' 'Sure is,' chorused the fellers, 'just great!' And assuring each other that they would have a ball on Simi, they lit cigars, opening dog-eared paperbacks and read extracts aloud to each other – long extracts. Gratuitously we were treated to unexpurgated passages from *Emanuelle* and heard that, in the opinion of the reader who had been baptised Hal, she was quite a doll and that he for one had never tried it that way; and from Waldo, his immediate companion, we were made privy to excerpts from the work of an author unknown to us entitled *Passion at the Lazy Y*, and which by now indubitably will have been remaindered. But it was Marvin who made the greatest cultural contribution.

51

By contrast with his well-fleshed, bareheaded friends, who were costumed in short-sleeved apparel which, like Jacob's coat, was of many colours, he wore a white T-shirt bearing the legend 'Moosehead Beer' in a green circle, blue shorts decorated with a large metal buckle, open sandals and a white ventilated cap. But most remarkable was his physique.

Tall and spare, with incredibly long thin limbs and a beaky nose upon which was perched a pair of small, round black sunglasses, he looked strikingly like a crane-fly. Somehow, one felt, he should have six legs instead of two, and that were he to present himself before a casting director of '*The Insect Play*' without question he would be hired as an extra. But as he revealed, he alone of the trio was a cognoscente of serious literature.

'Hey fellers!' he exclaimed, leaping from his seat in the manner of an excited daddy-long-legs and waving a travel book aloft. 'Do you guys know how Sigh-me gotten its name?' 'No,' said the fellers, 'we sure don't.' 'Well,' said Marvin, proceeding to make a Reader's Digest of the text before him, 'have you heard of a guy called Pro-mee-the-arse?' 'Pro who?' asked Waldo, looking blank. 'Mee-the-arse,' repeated Marvin impatiently, 'Pro-mee-the-arse.' 'Oh yeah,' said Hal reflectively, 'sure. Wasn't he a god, or sump'n?' 'That's right,' said Marvin showing pleasure at his friend's erudition, 'he sure was. And according to this guy,' he went on, jabbing at the open page, 'he lived on Sigh-me. And guess what, fellers?' He paused for effect. 'He found out that he could make people outa clay!' 'No kidding!' said Waldo. 'Yip,' confirmed Marvin, 'he sure did. But that ain't all fellers. Zous – now you know who Zous was, Waldo?' 'Oh sure,' said Waldo, relieved that he could redeem himself and rise from the bottom of the class, 'he was a kinda boss god, huh?' 'Correct,' said Marvin slapping his paperback. 'Ker-rect! Well now, he gotten sore at Pro-mee-the-arse. And fellers – guess what he did?' 'No idea,' said the fellers, and shook their heads. 'Well,' continued Marvin, 'he turned him into an ape! Yes sir, that's what he did – turned him into a ba-boon, *and* what's more, kept him on Sigh-me until he died.'

He paused again. 'Get it fellers? Sigh-me? Simayan? Ape!'

'Well wadya know,' said Waldo, 'Monkey Island!' 'Yeah,' said Hal, 'Planet of the Apes! Like on TV, huh? But get this bit from *Emanuelle* – and I tell you fellers she was no monkey – ha! Ha! Ha! Say, listen . . .'

And so it went on, an unrelieved corporate recital broken only when Waldo espied a zodiacal sign tattooed upon a nearby arm. 'Hey,' he cried to the owner of the limb, 'are you a Leo? Gee,' he volunteered, displaying his own similarly positioned insignia, 'I'm a Virgin! Gee, we're cosmic neighbours! Yeah, you're in one house and I'm right next door to you in the cosmos! What's your name, bud?' 'Alfred,' said the Lion in a strong German accent. 'Ah,' said Waldo, pinpointing his celestial brother's country of origin but affording him the title of King of Wessex, 'Alfred the Great! And you're a Kraut.' 'Yes', said the German mirthlessly, 'I am, as you say, a Kraut.' And mouthing a teutonic obscenity he turned his back, and moved away. 'Hey,' said Waldo, turning to his colleagues and opening his arms in pained inquiry, 'what's up with the guy? Did I say sump'n? 'No Waldo,' they said, employing double negatives, 'you didn't say nothin'.'

The two-hour journey passed quickly. Hard upon the all-American cabaret came the sights and sounds of two Greek grandmothers attempting but failing to expel their elevenses into cardboard boxes with the verve which only sea-going Greeks can muster, for'ard a party of young Simians returning to their island after the previous day's shopping spree on Rhodes sang to the accompaniment of a bouzoukoi, and down the companionway leading to the upper deck of the ferry came Stergos, the first mate.

'*Kali mera, Kirie* Yanni, *Kiria* Maria,' he called, surprising us by his use of the formal affixes of Mr and Mrs, 'Captain Vasili would like you to have a drink with him on the bridge and to watch our approach to Simi. 'We shall', he advised us, 'be there in thirty minutes you understand. *Endaxi?*' '*Ne,*' we said, '*Efharistume* – we thank you.' '*Malista,*' he said, and beckoned us to follow him aloft.

'*Ella pethia mou*', sang out Vasili as we arrived, and in sharp contrast to his mate's formality, 'come my children, my friends of Zagorianos – *ti tha puis?* What will you drink? Ouzo? Beer? *Cafe?*' 'Coffee,' we opted, 'Greek coffee. *Sketo* – without sugar.' '*Endaxi!*' he said, and relayed the order. 'But for myself I will take a little whisky. It is, you understand, for my stomach. *Ne*,' he enlarged, 'for many months now I have suffered from my stomach. *Mana mou*, how I have suffered! *Ne*, it is true, I cannot tell you the pain I have endured with my intestines.' He belched quietly, patted the afflicted region with his hand, apologised for his flatulence and reached for a bottle standing on a shelf below the vessel's compass. 'Ah,' he said, unscrewing the top and taking a swig, '*bravo* the Johnny Walker! Cheers!' '*Yasas,*' said Maria, '*ke perastika sou* - and get well!' '*Efharisto*,' said Vasili, and looked at her expectantly. 'Our friend Zagorianos tells me that you are a nurse, *ne*?' 'Yes,' said Maria, 'I am,' and resigned herself to giving another of the innumerable consultations which in Greece inevitably followed a disclosure of her calling. Ten minutes later and having treated us to a wholesale condemnation of Greek doctors in general, he thanked her profusely and we turned our attention to the scene ahead of us.

Before us, through the grime-encrusted window of the wheelhouse, the haze of distant land gradually grew more distinct as we ploughed toward it. 'So that,' I said, nodding in its direction, 'is Simi.' '*Oche*,' said Vasili taking the cups of thick black coffee from the deckhand who had delivered them and handing them to us, '*oche*. That is Turkey. *Ne*,' he repeated, 'Turkey,' and lapsed into English. 'Bloody Turkey,' he said, and spat.

'*Ne*,' he continued morosely, 'Simi is before us but she melts into the Turkish background you understand. *Ne*, almost as if she is frightened. And there,' he said, pointing to starboard, 'that also is Turkey. But look,' and turning around he directed us to a chart on the table behind him. 'You see,' he said, tracing the outlines of the Turkish mainland with his forefinger, 'it reaches out like a great jaw waiting to devour Simi, to gobble her up and take her into the Turkish belly. *Ne*, Maria, she hides like a woman afraid of being raped. And who knows,' he conjectured, 'perhaps she would be if we allowed it. And that, *pethia mou*, is why Greece must never turn its back on Turkey. Always we must be on guard.' He tapped the map before him and glared at me. 'I tell you Yanni, if ever you go to Turkey,' and here he crossed himself, 'which the God forbid, never let Maria out of your sight. *Mana mou*! They would ravage her over a cup of tea you understand? *Ne*! I would not even trust them with my favourite donkey!' And returning to his station he took another sip from his medicinal bottle. The dislike and mistrust of the Turks is never far below the surface in Greece; and particularly in the Dodecanese.

On we sailed. Simi divorced itself from the maw of Turkey as we neared it and we cruised northwards along its south-eastern coastline, pas the bays of Marathounta, Nanu and Ayios Disainas, the rocky mouthfuls which time and a hungry sea has clawed from the black, pitted flanks of the amoeba-shaped island, around the point of Cape Filonikos at the mouth of Ayios Nikolaus's bay which housed the tiny port of Pethi upon which in the coming days we were to look down from a villa set high in the rocky hills, and past an offshore islet graced by a whitewashed chapel. We watched it growing smaller in our wake and then, still wondering to which of the legions of saints it had been dedicated, rounded the Cape of Koutsoumpas and in a gentle, westerly arc began our approach to Gialos – 'one of the eight splendid ports of the island', so the Roman Pliny wrote – and to the old settlement of Simi.

Vasili offered us a binocular, and through the lenses the sizeable nineteenth-century town and the grey-green, craggy, volcanic hills above it sprang into sharp relief. We saw a long harbour crowded with an assemblage of fishing boats and caiques, some with bundled sponges hanging from their rigging, and one or two white-painted larger craft which plied their ways from island to island. To starboard a small stony beach the colour of pumice came into view, and before us a waterfront, above which tier upon tier of amber, white and sandstone-coloured houses with sloping tiled roofs of terracotta rose upon a hillside which, dotted with wedding-cake churches, leaned back and stretched up and up. And along the quay, as Yiorgo Zagorianos had said, *taverna* after *taverna*.

'*Ne*,' said Vasili, as we gave him a commentary on the panorama unfolding before us, '*ine orea, ne*? It is beautiful, yes? And peaceful too,' he added as he reclaimed the field glass, 'only a car or two, no buses, and once my sheep have left, few people. *Ne*, we shall return with them to Rhodes this afternoon you understand. Then you will have the place to yourselves with nothing to do but eat and sleep and walk and swim, and,' he leered, exercising his limited command of English once more, 'time in the beds together! Ha! Ha! *Endaxi* Yanni? *Endaxi* Maria?' And he nudged her in the ribs. '*Ne*,' he continued, but with greater delicacy, 'you will like it here,' and asked us where and for how long we were staying, and if we were being met. 'Ah,' he exclaimed when we advanced him the name of Zagorianos's friend who had been detailed to attend us on arrival, 'Nikos Pipsos. He too is a friend of mine. A good man – even when he is drunk. *Ne*, I will show him to you. But now you must excuse me – there is work. *Yasas!*'

We disembarked noisily and *en masse*. The jubilant returning islanders together with a goat, potatoes, assorted cheeses of varying ripeness plus a rich variety of other consumer goods which they had purchased in Rhodes were greeted warmly by friends and relatives; and so too were the ailing grandmothers. Still clasping their pristine cardboard boxes and, despite their earlier lack of success, continuing to give the impression that but a few minutes of life remained to them, they were embraced, unwillingly relieved of their emergency cartons, assisted to nearby packing-cases upon which they collapsed, and fed upon tangerines which, their nearest and dearest assured them, were the panacea for *mal de mer*, real or imagined. Meanwhile, the sheep, as Vasili unkindly had dubbed them, fanned out in chattering trios and quartets along the quay with their Nikons and Pentaxes working overtime. Some, the natural explorers of their number, eager for culture and new experiences, disappeared down alleyways and side streets; others, cajoled by beckoning waiters already on competitive alert outside *tavernas*, allowed themselves to be sucked into the premises forthwith; and Hal, Waldo and the Crane-fly were met by the proprietor of an apple-green and brown hotel on the sea front, given loud and extravagent assurances that it was indeed 'A' class, and shepherded to their Shangri-La with their luggage on a trolley. But of Nikos Pipsos, of whom Zagorianos had given us the briefest description, there was no sign; nor did Vasili manifest himself to effect the promised introduction.

Five long minutes later and harbouring the unworthy thought that perhaps Mr Pipsos was having a day on the grape and consequently suffering from temporary amnesia, a state of induced euphoria not uncommon among some Greek gentlemen resident in comparatively remote communities, Maria said: 'I think we ought to ask someone. There,' she said, nodding toward a benign-looking priest wearing dark glasses and employed in licking his index finger and counting a wad of drachmae, 'let's ask the *papas* – he's bound to know him.'

'*Ne! Ne! Ne!*' beamed that notable when we approached him and after we had exchanged civilities and he had established from where we had come, and why. 'Of course I know him. *Ne*' he confirmed, hoisting his robes and stuffing the offertory into his hip pocket, 'he is over there. You see?' And he pointed to a table at one of the quayside *tavernas*. '*Ne*, the thin man with the pinched face who is talking with the young pink couple with the peeling backs – that is Pipsos. But come, I will take you to him.' And putting one arm around Maria's waist and encircling mine with the other, he led the way.

'*Herete* Niko!' said the *papas* as we arrived at the table and startling our errant contact who appeared much on edge. 'Greetings! Here are two friends from Rhodes who have been looking for you. *Ne*, they came with the ferry you understand; and are hot – and,' he added, 'thirsty'.

57

'Ah!' exclaimed Nikos, leaping to his feet and kissing the *papas'* hand. '*Yasas, yasas!* And welcoom Mistaire Evdon. But,' he continued in mangled English, 'I was sorrowful not to have been at the foory when it brunged you. *Ne!* I have been er, how to say, emergencied. These people here,' he said, indicating the discomforted couple before him, 'have the problem and are angry with me. *Ne!* They say they are being er, er –'

'Buggered about,' said the pink male unpleasantly. 'That's what he's doing – buggering us about.' 'Yes,' endorsed his lady consort in a north London whine, 'we don't get what 'e's on about – know-watter-min?' '*Ne*,' said Nikos Pipsos agitatedly to the *papas*, '*ine etsi pater* – it is like that. That is the problem! It is my English!' 'Then why,' suggested his spiritual advisor, 'do you not tell *Kiri* Yannis of the affair and he will translate for you. *Mila ta Ellinika, katalavis* – he speaks Greek, you understand.'

'Ah,' said Nikos, raising his hands in thanksgiving for this divine inspiration, '*efharisto!* Thanks be to the God! I did not realise! *Bravo! Bravo!* And so saying, and lighting a fresh cigarette, he related the saga to us.

'This couple', he appraised us, 'are troublesome. *Ne! Poli.* They wish a room, you understand; a room with a view,' he elaborated, reminding us of the late Sir Noel Coward. 'But,' he continued, 'I am telling them that accommodation here is limited, and that there are problems. A room with a lovely view, I tell them, is possible – but without water. And the rooms with water have no lovely views. So what can I do, I say? they cannot have both – and I tell them so. I say either you wash and have no scenery, or you look at the sea and get filthy; but that I say, is up to you. *Terma* – finish! And now, *Kiri* Yanni, translate, please.'

I did so. there was a short silence eventually broken by the pink male. 'Codswallop!' he said. 'Yer,' echoed his friend, but more briefly, '**balls!** Why isn't there no wau'er?' I relayed the question. 'Because,' said Nikos drumming his fingers on the table top and looking to the *papas* for support, 'it is one of our hazards. There is little water on the island – only that from the rain which we store in tanks. And if the mayor says no more water today, or tomorrow, it is like that. *Ne*,' he repeated, 'just like that', and he shrugged his shoulders. '*Ne*,' agreed the *papas*, 'it is the same on Nimos where I live, just across the bay. And if the God sends little rain there is much trouble. This you must tell these children.'

Once again I donned my interpreter's hat. The news was not well received. 'Well,' said the girl, 'it didn't say nothink about that in me brocher, did it, Vic?' 'No it bloody never', said Vic belligerently and rising to his feet. 'An' I tell yer something else too, mate, I can't stand no more of this sodding jabbering neither. 'Ere, come on Nirene, let's . . . orf back to Rhodes?' 'Yer,' said Nirene, 'we'll do just that.' And hoisting their backpacks painfully on to their shoulders they slouched out of our lives.

Nikos gazed after them with relief. 'Thanks be to the God for that,' he breathed. 'They were not very pleasant people. But tell me please,' he inquired, jerkily stubbing out his cigarette, 'what is this phrase "boogeredaboud"?' '*Ne*,' echoed the *papas*, 'I too was puzzled.'

It was not easy but I enlightened them. 'Po! Po! Po!' said the *papas*. 'Such coarseness.' '*Ne*,' agreed Nikos, 'but useful. Boogeredaboud', he repeated, relishing the sound. '*Ne*, I will remember it. But now,' he said, abruptly ending the tutorial, '*pame* – we go.' And jumping up like a jack-in-the-box he seized our cases and indicated a faded blue and rusty Nissan pick-up standing in full sun by the ferry. 'That', he said, 'is mine. *Ella!* Come!'

'*Tipota*,' said the *papas* as *en route* for the jaded vehicle we thanked him for his help, 'don't mention it. But come and see me on my island. It is not very beautiful but there is a small beach where you can take your clothes off. *Ne!* – all of them! *Endaxi* Maria? Come and do that thing – but leave Yannis behind, *ne*? Ho! Ho! Ho!' And wishing us to go to the good, he waved us goodbye.

Even in the short while we had become acquainted with

Nikos Pipsos we had formed the opinion that he was of a nervy disposition and his driving did little to alter our diagnosis. For what seemed an eternity, and leaving a swirling dust-cloud behind us, we climbed and bounced over an uneven hard-packed earthen road which, hugging the edges of precipitous cliffs, wound upward like a yellow snake with the sea below us. Corners came and corners went, each greeted with a squeal of well-worn brakes, and stones showered seaward as our wheels clipped the side of the roadway. It was not the heat of the cab alone which brought us out in beads of perspiration: it was fear.

Silently we sat huddled on the bench seat, our throats drying and our nails biting deeper into each other's palms. 'Is it not beautiful?' yelled Nikos attempting to change from second gear to first but having an unfortunate encounter with neutral on the way. 'Is it not wonderful, the view?' '*Ne*,' we said over the screech of the protesting gear-box, 'truly splendid', and closed our eyes to the scene. Fifteen minutes later, and believing even more fervently in the efficacy of prayer, we arrived.

'*Ella!*' cried Nikos, leaping from the cab and darting round to the back to fetch our luggage. 'That is your house!' And pointing to the third and highest of three small flat-roofed modern villas with wooden shutters he led the way up a steep shaley path toward it.

'*Endaxi!*' he said, unceremoniously dumping the cases on the tiled floor of the twin-bedded room and mopping his brow. '*Ine kala, ne?*' '*Poli Kala*,' said Maria inspecting the general furnishings and the combined shower and lavatory, 'very good.' '*Ne*,' agreed Nikos, flushing the cistern to prove that it worked and looking relieved when it did so, 'but *please*,' he implored as the water rose quickly to seat-level and spilled over the rim, 'no papers down the toilet.' 'No! No! No! Of course not!' we chorused, well versed in the ways of Greek plumbing and watching the reluctant departure of the flood in a frenzy of evil-smelling bubbles, 'always the bucket. *Ne*,' said Nikos beaming appreciatively and enthusiastically working the foot-pedal of the adjacent orange plastic bin, 'always the bucket.

Ne, Ireni from the store will empty it for you every other day. That is,' he added hastily, 'if she remembers. She has, you understand many problems; but she is a good person. *Ne,*' he continued speeding us into the tiny kitchenette, 'see what she has done!' And jerking open the door of the refrigerator he disclosed its contents.

'There!' he said triumphantly. 'Look! Cheese, yoghurt, bread, and,' he said, completing the itinerary and seizing two bottles and waving them aloft with the air of a conjurer producing a rabbit from a hat, 'retsina! *Ne!* Just to welcome you! And when they are finished you go to her supermarket for more. It is quite close you understand – just up the hill. But now,' he concluded, urgently replacing the bottles and slamming the refrigerator door behind them, 'I must leave. *Yasu* Maria! *Yasu* Yanni! *Harika poli* – I am pleased to have met you. You will, I think, be happy here. *Ne,*' he said, making his way quickly to the little veranda and turning at the top of the short spiral flight of steps leading to the pathway below, 'here you will not be – ha! ha! – **boogeredaboud**! *Andio!*'

'I am sure,' said Maria as we watched him go, 'that we won't. But,' said she, availing herself of three saucepans and a beaker from the pine kitchen cupboard and moving towards the taps, 'one never knows when the mayor may strike. Remember Kadamena?' she reminded me as she filled the receptacles and a washing-up bowl in the sink, 'And Karpathos?' 'Indeed I do,' I said drawing on past and horrid memories when we had been left waterless on other islands, 'and Nisyros.'

We took stock of our surroundings. Through a fly-infested window at the end of the bedroom we looked down upon a derelict stone house with crumbling walls and to a narrow street which, as we discovered later, was one of a maze of lanes leading to Ireni's supermarket. But from the square verandah the view was more salubrious.

Way below us on our left, with the south-eastern port of Pethi hidden from our sight, was the keyhole-shaped Gulf of Ayios Nikolaus across whose mouth we had passed on the ferry, and on the skyline the landmass of Turkey. To the

61

east of the bay the olive-shaped land sloped irregularly down to the sea, and at our backs and beyond a grey dry-stone wall surmounted by a rusty wire-netting fence, against which a mongrel bitch on heat rubbed her rump in ecstasy, more boulder-strewn hills rose over a valley in the lee of which was a scattering of white houses and a large church with a turmeric dome.

'*Yasas!*' called a little girl, waving to us from the doorway of one of two pink houses flanking the narrow pathway between us, and asked us from where we had come, how long we were staying, and what our names were. So too did her mother, her sister and a disabled aunt dressed in black. 'Ah,' cried the crippled one, 'that is good! I too am a Maria – and so is the child! *Ne!* And my husband, *krima sto palikari* – may the earth rest light upon him – he was a Yannis like you. *Bravo! Bravo!*' And so our first contacts were made. We were advised what we could buy at Ireni's and when she was open; that her daughter Nikoletta was a beautiful girl but no good at sums; how we could get to Simi port in no time at all without using the steps through the town but that we should wait until the sun got lower, and that meanwhile we should have a meal and a good wash in case the water ran out.

Minutes later, and as we were acting upon their advice, there was a tap on the glass-panelled door of the bedroom. '*Parakalo* – please,' lisped little Maria, and presented us with a bowl of eggs and a huge plateful of beans. '*Parakalo*,' she repeated as we thanked her, and ran giggling down the steps to her mother. '*Tipota*,' called the latter in response to our shouted gratitude, '*kali oreksi* – good appetite – they were laid this morning!'

They were kind and generous neighbours but not, as we were made aware, guides *par excellence*. We did walk to Simi in the mid-afternoon but not, it transpired, by their recommended scenic route.

'Po! Po! Po!' exclaimed an unshaven ancient with bow legs and a knobbly olive walking-stick whom we met on our way and who asked us where we were going. 'You must be mad my children. *Ne*, demented – *parafron*! *Mana mou*, I have known donkeys to be crippled on that track. *Ne*, they have laid down in the road and died, you understand? *Oche*,' he crackled, waving his stick in the direction of the upper town, 'you go that way. *Ne*! Down the many steps in the usual manner and you will be in Gialos in fifteen minutes. *Endaxi*?' '*Endaxi*,' we said, meekly, and went on our way leaving him still muttering about dying donkeys and the follies of bipeds who took that path.

Still heavy with luncheon beans upon which unwisely we had fallen with relish, but grateful for our informant's fortuitous intervention, like mountain goats we picked our way down the steep, sloping, narrow cobbled streets of the oldest settlement on the island; past shuttered shops and dozing dogs oblivious to the urgent flies; past *cafeneons*, their owners comatose at siesta time; past the *archontika* – the grander buildings which stood as monuments to the aristocrats of two hundred years ago when Simi enjoyed its heyday as a trading centre; down steps, straight and spiral, across short stone landings and down, down, down more steps until at last we reached the Skala, a small square next to the quay.

Gingerly Maria felt her calves. 'I don't know about you,' she said, 'but I made it three hundred and sixty-five.' 'Three hundred and sixty-five what?' I asked. 'Steps,' she said, continuing to apply the massage, 'steps.'

By contrast with the inertia of the upper town the port was a hive of industry and still patronised by the day-trippers who, in varying stages of euphoria or disarray, were waiting to embark upon their return journey to Rhodes. And seated at a table by the ferry booking office was Vasili. '*Yassas*!' he called out, waving us over to him. '*Katse, katse* – sit down, sit down. A coffee perhaps?' '*Ne*,' we said, grateful for the opportunity to rest our legs and mindful of the statutory glasses of cold water which would accompany it, '*efharistume*,' and told him of our adventures.

'Ah,' he laughed, 'the steps, the steps, the famous steps! *Ne*! But they get steeper at night you understand. *Mana mou*, how steep they become after a bottle or two! *Ne*,' he fantasised, 'there is, in my opinion, a man who lives at the top of the village, the very demon of a man you understand, a *diavolos* who has them on a string! And he pulls and pulls at these steps until they are almost vertical. And the more retsina one has to drink, the harder he pulls! *Ne, sosta* – it is true!' And he slapped his knee and roared with laughter, and lit a cigarette.

'But seriously,' he continued, inhaling and then expelling the smoke, 'unless you wish it there is no need to punish your legs and come down here to eat. *Oche*! There are two quite good *tavernas* much nearer to you. And on the road to Pethi there is a *cafeneon*. *Ne, Lefteris* there is a friend of mine, he will look after you. And,' he added, with one eye on a crew member who was checking the tickets of the boarding passengers, 'do not come here for the swimming.' He drew on his cigarette again and gesticulated toward a hobbling walking-wounded. 'You see that unfortunate there?' he asked. 'Do you know what he has done? *Oche*? Well, I will tell you. He has, my friends, trodden on an *ahinos* – a sea urchin. *Ne*,' he enlarged, as the parrotless Long John Silver limped onto the ferry, 'the rocks are alive with them round here. Better you go, I think, to Ayios Thomas. It is a little bay you understand not far from Pethi and the water is clean and deep there. *Ne*, I will show you.' And sketching the route on the back of his empty Karelia packet he gave it to Maria. '*Etsi*,' he said, 'like that. But now,' he concluded, rising and stretching as the last of the excursionists straggled through the open stern of the ferry, 'it is time for me to return my sheep to the fold, although,' he added, flicking his half-smoked cigarette away, 'to my mind it is possible that some of them will not know when they arrive.' And he laughed. '*Andio*,' he said, 'pray for my stomach, Maria,' and he walked slowly toward the vessel.

Together with a knot of other people, we watched them depart waving shirts, hats, arms and towels form both sides of the boat while a section of the English contingent who, we suspected had only seen Simi from the inside of a *taverna*, treated us to untuneful renderings of 'We'll Meet Again' and, for some totally illogical reason, 'We Shall Not Be Moved'. '*Ne*,' said a fat man next to us as we joined in the reciprocal messages being shouted across the water, '*kathimerinos ine etsi* – daily it is like this. *Alla*,' he continued, '*tora ine isychia, ne?* Now it is peaceful?' '*Ne*,' we agreed, 'it is better like this.' '*Bori*,' said the fat one, 'perhaps. But it is good for business when they come!' And patting his hip pocket he chuckled, and moved away.

For a while we sauntered around the by now all but deserted streets and then leisurely made our way to the opposite side of the horseshoe bay. In front of one of the several fine neo-classical houses facing the pumice-grey beach we had seen to starboard on our approach to Gialos was a mooring platform festooned with old motor tyres, and upon the edge of it were Hal, Waldo and Marvin. Hal was standing with his hands on his hips, Waldo was lying down with one foot in the air, and Marvin was addressing himself to the sole of it with a pair of eyebrow tweezers.

'Urchins,' volunteered Hal as we approached the trio, 'goddam sea urchins, dozens of the bastards.' 'Yip,' confirmed Marvin eliciting a yelp from the supine Waldo as he plucked out another spine, 'sure are. Right down there ma'am', he advised Maria. 'Go see, the both of you.'

We did so. And as we peered into the shallow depths to the grey-green slimy rocks upon which their prickly tormentors were clustered, a very dead cat, attended by half a dozen flower petals and looking remarkably like a feline Ophelia, floated slowly past us from left to right, gently bobbing as it went.

'Holy cow!' breathed Hal pushing his sun hat to the back of his head and following the passage of the drifting corpse with his eyes out on stalks. 'This I do not *believe*! Hey fellers, look! A *mog*', he expostulated. 'A dead, floatin' mog! Well, wadya know!' 'Yeah,' said the fellers as they gazed transfixed, 'wadya know. Gee!'

'I think', said Maria in an undertone as Marvin returned to his life's work on the punctured Waldo and after we had

Holy cow! . . . A mog! . . . A dead floatin' mog!

offered them our condolences, 'that Vasili was right.' 'Yes,' I agreed, as we set off for home, 'I'm sure he was.' But Vasili was right on another score. There *was* a demon on the top of the hill. Moreover, he did not wait until nightfall to exercise his powers. He stretched the steps with his magic rope at five o'clock that afternoon, increasing the gradient by a factor of two and doubling our walking time back to the villa. 'Ah,' said our neighbours, observing our halting progress up the concrete steps, having seen us approach from the opposite direction to their suggested route, 'did we not tell you to go the other way? Did we not tell you so? Po! Po! Po!' And shaking their heads they went inside to deliberate upon our foolishness.

Mercifully, the mayor was in good humour that evening. We soaked our bleeding, swollen feet in the washing-up bowl, watched them assume their normal colour and size, showered gratefully under intermittent sprays of lukewarm water and then, relaxing in chairs upon the veranda with Ireni's retsina and olives we had brought from Rhodes, waited for the day to die.

The sun goes down more hastily in Greece than it does in an English sky, and that soft, caressing period of twilight – the dimsey as they still call it in parts of Devon – is shorter. Above us in the fading light, the unrequited tethered bitch still stropped her backside against the wire-netting fence, whimpering with pleasure as she did so; below us in an empty house two plasterers sang one to the other, their voices echoing around the room in which they worked; a flock of sparrows, twittering in anticipation of the encroaching night, hurtled in urgent undulating flight toward an olive tree to roost; and together we watched the sea and the hills turn to purple, and the gentle merging of the land and sea; and I thought of Bunyan's lines on the 'Going Down of the Sun':

What, hast thou run thy race? Art going down?
Thou seemest angry, why dost thou frown?
Yea wrap thy head with clouds, and hide thy face,
As leaving to withdraw from us thy Grace?

Oh leave us not! When once thou hid'st thy head,
Our Horizon with darkness will be spread.
Tell's who hath thee offended? Turn again;
Alas! too late. Entreaties are in vain . . .

Somewhere in the distance a dog howled and was answered by another from across the valley, and then another. The plasterers left the building and still singing made their way toward the upper slopes of the village; and onomatopoeically an owl hooted its Grecian name, '*koo-koo-vaya, koo-koo-vaya.*' Gradually the sparrows in the olive tree grew quieter until only solo cheeps reached us from within its branches, and one by one in the gathering darkness dull spots of light began to dot the hillsides and the valley. Night came to Simi.

For an hour we sat there saying little and listening to the unseen cicada orchestra tuning up, but we did not go down to Gialos again. Nor did we seek out Vasilis's friend Lefteris on the road to Pethi. We did not go anywhere. Our spirits were willing and our stomachs keen but as we discovered when we attempted to rise, our lower limbs thought otherwise. 'Enough!' they cried, 'we can take no more!' and knotted their muscles in protest. But, as we consoled ourselves before hobbling stiff-legged to our beds, there are worse things on which to sup than eggs and beans . . . and retsina.

5

Simi Remembered

It was not the lark but church bells which awoke us at half past six next morning, bells from many belfries. Tenors and trebles clanged and peeled both high and low, vying one with the other in a frenzied tintinabulation to usher in Saturday and rouse us from our sleep.

I yawned, stretched, indulged in all the rites performed by awakening Homo sapiens, sluiced my face and went out on to the verandah. Beyond the narrow inlet to the bay, Turkey lay hidden in the early morning mist, and the sea as yet unkissed by the rays of the sun was smooth and nondescript in colour. A slight breeze ruffled the leaves of the olive tree making them whisper with pleasure, and near at hand a donkey brayed loud and long and brassily like a tanker's siren. In the far distance a cock crowed and was answered stridently by another arrogantly standing on the path below me, its chest puffed out, its crimson comb and wattles shaking with affronted pride. And from a hillside came the tinkling of goat bells as the herds began to graze.

'Dong-dong, dong-dong' clanged the deep tenor bell from the church on the hill. 'Dang-dang, dang-dang' said a distant treble, and 'ting-ting-ting' said another; and with the passing of the minutes the light grew stronger. But the magic of a post-dawn Grecian morning was yet to come and I stood there in anticipation looking eastwards and toward the mythological past, waiting . . . awaiting the moment when Helios in his chariot of gold, fashioned by Hephaestus and drawn by nine winged horses, their nostrils issuing fire and smoke, would leave the swamps in the far-off land of the Ethiopians, charge through the gates of dawn and climb the vault of heaven.

It was seven fifteen when the huge deep orange orb, the day star as William Blake called it, climbed swiftly over the brow of the hills and splashed the tops and upper slopes with molten gold. It touched a solitary white fleecy cloud, tinging its leading edge with flamingo pink; it reached into the hollows and chased away the shadows; and it turned the sea into a mirror of shot silk. Not for the first time in my life I thanked God for the inestimable gift of sight.

'*Kali mera Yanni,*' called Maria senior, breaking my thoughts as she limped into her tiny courtyard armed with a blue plastic bowl full of washing and attended by three half-grown cats, 'and did you sleep well?' '*Ne,*' I answered, '*poli kala efharisto. Ke sis? -* and you?' Maria tilted her eyebrows and clicked her tongue in an unspoken negative. '*Oche,*' she endorsed, 'I had the wind. *Ne,*' she elaborated with that engaging frankness exampled by every Greek when embarking upon matters pertinent to their physical state, and as her namesake joined me on the verandah, 'every night I suffer from the wind you understand. *Poli, poli.*' And she sighed and pegged out a pillowcase. 'But tell me,' she continued, her train of thought possibly subconsciously motivated by her last statement, 'did you enjoy the beans last night? We know you did not go out again you understand. *Ne,*' she volunteered, adding a hand-towel to the line, 'I said to Erasmeia, those children will not go out with feet as swollen as theirs I said. *Ne,* I said, they will stay inside and eat our beans and do nothing but sleep. But,' she pursued, bending and selecting another item from the bowl and involuntarily exampling her discomforture, '*did* you enjoy them?' '*Ne,*' I assured her, '*itane poli nostimi*' – they were extremely tasty and', I added, 'filling.' '*Ne,*' said my Maria, 'very filling.' '*Bravo!*' beamed Maria senior, well pleased with the success of the offering and kicking a cat off the laundry. 'Then I will bring you some more. *Ne!* Now! For your breakfast!' and she made to move toward the house.

Maria pressed her foot upon mine. 'Ah,' I said, taking the hint and equally conscious that protein-packed though beans may be, they can, and often do produce explosive and

70

unsociable side-effects when eaten to excess, *'efharistume para poli*, but we were just going up to Ireni's: to buy yoghurt,' I enlarged.

Maria frowned. *'Yaoorti?'* she repeated. *'Yaoorti?'* 'Ne,' I confirmed, *'yaoorti*. It is', I explained, 'very good for breakfast. Especially that which is made from sheep's milk.' Maria's frown deepened. 'Possibly,' she conceded, 'but in my opinion beans are better. Three times a day I eat beans, you understand. *Ne*, they are most nourishing. However . . .', and shrugging her shoulders she hung out a pair of patched longjohns, kicked the cat again for good measure, and went indoors. 'Oh dear,' I said, as she banged the door shut, 'I think we're out of favour.' 'Never mind,' said Maria. 'I'll give her some bismuth later on. That at least should give her one night's respite.' 'Yes,' I said, 'and presumably the rest of the family as well. Anyway, let's go.'

It took us five minutes to arrive at Ireni's emporium at the top of the hill. We reached it via a maze of narrow back streets graced with purple bougainvillaea and blue potato creepers which cascaded over balconies and walls, our progress meticulously logged by five little girls, two old ladies washing their doorsteps and a one-eared cat dismembering a locust. All, save the cat, wished us good morning, all asked us where we were going and the children, laughing and dancing and skipping before us, showed us the way. 'There it is,' they cried as we halted before the double wooden doors of the building, 'this is Ireni's!' And still chattering and giggling they ran back into the labyrinth of streets.

Ireni's was a large establishment with the external appearance of a warehouse rather than that of a shop. Inside, to the left of the doors, were sacks of grain and fertilisers, drums of olive oil and diesel fuel, and the rusting parts of an outboard engine. To the right were packing cases piled high with vegetables. Tired tomatoes begging to be bought hobnobbed with polished aubergines and peppers, and above them drunken shelves precariously held bottles of wine, ouzo and other elixirs. In the corner, next to a flagpole wrapped with a

furled Greek standard, a vast, old-fashioned, overworked
refrigerator noisily hummed its frozen song to a mound of
Calor gas containers cohabiting with tins of Nescafé; before
us a long, glass-fronted, refrigerated display cabinet housed
cheeses, yoghurt, imported meats and other perishables, and
beyond this centrepiece mops, storm lanterns, brooms and
bundled wooden shafts for hoes hung from the rafters in
the dim abyss.

Sitting on a wooden chair in front of the counter and being
watched by three girls in their early teens was a very old lady
tenderly being fed on bread and milk by a spare, hook-nosed
old man with a white clipped moustache, and wearing a
Panama hat. '*Bravo Yaya!*' cried the jean-clad trio encouragingly as another sop was accepted from the spoon, 'well done
Granny!' And they chattered one to the other and said how
sweet she was. Laboriously, uncertainly, the old lady raised
her head, and slowly her eyes, violet and rheumy with age, lit
up with pleasure. 'Ne,' she mouthed gummily, drawing back
her lips in a toothless smile, '*ine kala.*' And from behind the
counter, her elbows resting upon its top and her chin cupped
in her hands, Ireni, together with her innumerate daughter
Nikoletta, fondly eyed the ancients.

She was a short, dark-haired, olive-skinned homely soul
in her mid-forties with thick black eyebrows and, as was
revealed when she left the shelter of the counter to greet us,
well endowed if not well balanced. 'Ah!' she exclaimed, her
face breaking into a broad smile of welcome and displaying
a gold-encrusted pre-molar as she came quickly toward us.
'*O Yannis ke e Maria, ne? Kalos! Kalos!*' she said, shaking
us warmly by the hand and beckoning to her daughter to do
likewise. '*Cafe?*' And instructing Nikoletta to bring two more
chairs she motioned us to sit down next to the aged couple.
'My parents,' she said by the way of introduction, and affec-
tionately stroked her father's gaunt white-bristled cheek. 'He
too is a Yanni,' she said.

With the ghost of a smile, slowly the old man nodded
in agreement. '*Ne,*' he quavered, shakily offering his wife a

. . . being tenderly fed on bread and milk . . .

final *bonne-bouche* and giving the empty bowl to Ireni. *'Barba Yanni?'* Grey, sunken but surprisingly alert eyes looked at me from under bushy brows of the same colour. *'Exeris 'Barba Yanni'* Yanni?' he inquired. *'Ne,'* I laughed, remembering the age-old folk-song of that title relating the exploits of a dirty old man with an eye for the girls; and started to sing it to him. 'Ah,' he wheezed, *'bravo* Yanni,' and patted me gently on my knee. 'But tell me, how old are you?' 'Fifty-seven,' I said; 'and you?' 'Po! Po! Po!' said Ireni as Nikoletta appeared with the coffee, 'No-one knows! There were no documents when he was born, you understand. Perhaps he has ninety years, perhaps a hundred even – who knows except the God?' And she laughed and bent down to give him a kiss. *'Thenbirazi,'* she said, squeezing his hand, 'it does not matter. He still has a mind and not cobwebs in his head and can talk of when he was young. *Ne,* he was once, you understand, a sponge-fisher – is that not so *Papa?'*

Momentarily the old man met her eyes, lingered on them, then dropped his lids. *'Ne,'* he husked, *'ine sosta* – it is true.' He paused, willing the past to enter the present. Then, as it did so, he turned his gaze on me. 'But that, you must understand,' he said, 'was many, many years ago. *Ne,* maybe fifty, sixty or even more, when the island had more people than it has today and we dived for sponges to make our living – to fill our bellies you understand.' And he stared into the middle distance and smiled as the recollections flooded in.

'Mana mou!' he reminisced. 'How we dived when we were young! *And* proved to the girls how strong we were! *Ne,* stronger even than the men of Kalymnos who also dived. They were good but we were better. *Ne,* much better.' He paused again, then redirected his attention once more to me. 'But there was, my friend, a reason. In those days if a man could not dive to thirty metres, he was not allowed to marry. *Ne, etsi itan pethi mou* – that's how it was, my child.' And he coaxed a chuckle from his chest and laid his hand upon my wrist. *'Katalavis?'* he said. 'You understand?'

'Ah,' said Ireni, speaking of her father as though he was

absent, 'so many things he remembers on his good days; but he cannot do much for himself, or for my mother. *Ne*,' she explained, addressing Maria as woman-to-woman, 'there is much work: much washing you understand, as if for babies. *Ne*, so many sheets and other articles each day. Po! Po! Po!' And she lifted her eyes to the roof and sighed. 'But there,' she said, lovingly looking at her parents; '*mi chirotera* – it could be worse. And the children help of course . . .'

It is not easy to shop quickly in rural Greece. An hour on, much later than we had anticipated, and further delayed by Nikoletta's inability to add up our bill correctly – a problem compounded by the intervention of the teenagers who individually produced three different totals – we left, clutching our provisions, and returned to the villa to breakfast off the despised yogurt and to mull over the unexpected insight into the sometime physical prowess of the Simian male. And, as we had done on other occasions, we reflected yet again on the unity of Greek family life, which had been manifested at Ireni's. The Greeks may not have the buffer of the welfare state as we know it, but within their households the elderly are respected, loved and cared for by the younger generation and not looked upon as burdens. In the Greek islands more than lip service is paid to the Fifth Commandment of Moses. As Maria said, as we set out for Captain Vasili's recommended swimming venue near Pethi, '*here* fathers and mothers *are* honoured.'

'*Yasu!*' called little Maria nursing one of the delinquent cats as we passed her gate. '*Poo parte* – where are you going?' '*Sto* Ayios Thomas,' we told her, and returning her wave turned right and cut across a patch of waste ground to meet the downhill road to Pethi.

Already tacky in the growing heat it was an unremarkable stretch of tarmac which, once it had curved past a cluster of humble houses at its highest point, ran in an almost unbroken line through sloping scrubland dotted with gorse, oregano, various cacti, and the stunted limbs of old and dying wattle and olive trees. Perched upon the blackening branches of one such specimen and at head height near the verge, a

bored-looking owl, ignoring our greeting, eyed us unblinkingly as we passed by, and from a solitary roadside *taverna*
to our right, which we identified as that belonging to Vasili's
friend Lefteris, an emaciated mongrel dog loped forward and
passed us with a lolling tongue and wearing an idiot smile.
Of the blue-washed establishment's incumbent there was no
sign, but the sound of breaking glass from within it followed
by a stream of invective suggested that he was in residence if
not in the best of humours.

'I think', murmured Maria as another heavy fall of glass
assaulted our ears and the unseen blasphemer screamed afresh
and hit top C, 'that we'll introduce ourselves on the way back.'
'Yes,' I said, as we followed a bend in the road and passed a
shuffling black-draped crone bent double under a pannier of
prickly pears, 'perhaps that would be best.'

Pethi port was not a hive of industry. Indeed, Pethi port
appeared to be as alive as its nearby necropolis; and less well-
cared-for. A cargo ship of imprecise tonnage, its superstructure
in urgent need of paint and innocent of activity, was moored
alongside the concrete quay; one or two small fishing boats
bobbed lazily in the shallows; at the water's edge an elderly
man in a dark blue jersey and matching hat gazed unseeingly
at an unresponsive red-painted float; and behind him, in the
shelter of a plastered wall fronting a double-storeyed blue-
painted Venetian building, a monstrous ginger tomcat, its right
leg slanted over its left shoulder like an abandoned anti-aircraft
gun, pursued its exploration of its privy parts and its hunt for
hidden fleas. Thus engrossed, it took scant notice of us, not
even when we called 'Puss Puss' and asked it how it was; nor
did a besotted tourist couple sucking Seven Up through twin
straws stuck into a communal can. Under the rush canopy of
a little beach *taverna* they had no eyes for anyone but each other. Indulgently we smiled upon them, remembering the days
when the world had stood still for us, and skirting its bamboo
fence crunched over the rocky shore, its stones slippery with
weed and algae, gingerly we picked our way to the beginning
of a snaking goat track on the hillside.

Up and up we climbed in the shadow of the shaley heights above us, then down and down and up again, the encroaching gorse on the sides of the trail scratching and needling our bare legs as we clambered. A hare, startled by our approach, sprang from its cover and ran with flattened ears in a zig-zag. course ahead of us before leaping back into the anonymity of the brush; tiny lizards with turquoise tails and similarly disturbed scuttled in panic across our path, and overhead a hawk, its tail extended downward in a fan, hovered against the wind on quickly beating wings and quartered the slopes in search of prey.

On we stumbled. Around yellow lichen-covered boulders, over stones honed to a razor's edge which cut into our shoes, past scatterings of rabbit droppings and spent cartridge cases, until after half an hour's trekking we stood breathless upon a promontory and from a height of fifty feet or so looked down upon the little whitewashed monastery of Ayios Thomas. As Vasili had told us, it stood on the fringes of arid amber-coloured hills and upon a gently curving pebble beach studded with clumps of dusty green almirithra trees only a few feet separating it from the rocky shallows of the bay of Ayios Nikolaos. And, as Vasili had promised us, there was not a soul to be seen. It was a pleasing prospect and for a moment or two we stood there, enjoying it in silence. Then Maria spoke. 'Look!' she said, and pointed to the far end of the cove. There, more immediately compelling, more urgently inviting than the memorial residence to the late Saint Thomas, was a short concrete mooring built into the foot of an escarpment, and three feet below it was deep, crystal clear, aquamarine water.

It had been a long, hot and tiring haul, and as the perspiration ran into our eyes and our shirts clung stickily to our backs, we knew our first objective. Hand in hand, clammily and cautiously we side-stepped down the ragged slope, digging in our heels for purchase and suffering further minor lacerations as we descended, trudged past the chapel and so to our journey's end. And there, safe in the knowledge that we could offend no person, we stripped off our clothes, dived naked into the warm clear water, and rejoiced.

For a while we swam, heads down and enchanted by the beauty of the marine world below us. We saw fan-shaped opalescent shells, magnified by the depth of water to the size of dinner plates shining from their resting places on the sea-bed; shoals of tiny fish playing follow-my-leader through gently waving weeds of many colours, coruscating as they flicked and turned as a single unit in obedience to a secret command; and a solitary octopus half-hidden in the cleft of a rock. Then, hoisting ourselves from the water and using our knapsacks as pillows, we lay upon the jetty to soak up the sun and listen to the lazy lapping of the sea against the wall. And as Yeats would have had it, 'peace came dropping slow.'

Twice, a panic-stricken shoal of small fishes pursued by an unseen predator took to the air for a dozen yards then broke the flat surface again in a flurry of fins and spray, a pied crow called hoarsely from a nearby crag, but little else disturbed our meditations. Then, unexpectedly, the sea whispered to us.

It was a whisper which second by second grew stronger and stronger, and raising ourselves on our elbows we watched the placid waters rise and swell as the billows set up by the wash of a passing ferry on its way to Pethi nudged the far end of the beach. Inexorably they rolled across the bay gaining strength and momentum as they came, the approaching murmur growing to a mutter and then to a roar like that of a cup-final crowd at Wembley stadium, and I shouted to Maria: 'Poseidon comes! And he's angry!' Then, just as dramatically, the noise subsided as the tired waves, drained of energy after their climactic effort, died on the shingle and gurgled their death rattles among the black honeycombed rocks; and silence came once more – but not for long.

In the aftermath of this display of tidal petulance came the distant phut-phut-phut of an outboard engine, and looking across to Pethi we watched a dot on the waters quickly grow larger and then resolve itself into a motorised rowing-boat as it steered towards us. 'I think,' said Maria, handing me my underpants and shorts and draping herself with a towel, 'that we are about to have visitors.' 'Yes,' I said inadvertently putting both feet through the same leg-hole of my Y-fronts and wincing slightly as hastily I corrected the error, 'and very shortly.'

My judgement was accurate. Two minutes later, and hard upon my victory over a malfunctioning zip, the small craft with a bearded man at the tiller and carrying a couple in their early thirties, together with a pop-eyed toddler plugged with a dummy, and an overweight bespectacled grandmother wearing grey stockings and a floral print cotton dress, glided to a halt beside us and landed its passengers.

'*Kali meres*,' they said acknowledging our greetings as they unloaded a basket, a push-chair and divers other picnic accessories, at our feet. 'You must be English, *ne*?' '*Ne*,' we confirmed, 'But how did you guess?' The boatman laughed and tapped the side of his nose. 'Because', he explained, 'you put on your clothes. We could see you were undressed, you understand. Had you been Germans you would not have shown concern for us. '*Ne*,' agreed Grandma, adjusting her errant knee-high hose and hoisting the little one on to her hip, 'that is so. They are shameless and show everything. But how did you get here?' 'We walked', we said, 'from the village.' '*Mana mou!*' said Blackbeard good-humouredly as the younger man passed him money, 'then you are not only English, but English goats! For sixty drachs I would bring you here, and take you back to Pethi with unblistered feet. *Thenbirazi!* Another time perhaps. *Andio kosta ke efharisto.*' And pocketing the notes he restarted the engine, wished his clients a happy day, confirmed that he would pick them up at four o'clock and throbbed away.

'*Yasas*,' said the trio, waving their free hands to us as we returned to our prone positions, and following in the waddling wake of Grandma wandered to the end of the jetty, crossed before the grey, five-arched collonade fronting the chapel and set up camp under the trees to the left of it.

Very properly the women unpacked, spread and anchored

a tablecloth upon the ground with gathered stones; and very properly the head of the household lit a cigarette, lay flat upon his back, and did nothing. Grandma, encouragingly and sibilantly saying '*pee-pee-pee*' to her granddaughter, took the child to below the furthest tree, held her hopefully a foot above the ground and waited, while Mother, vanishing behind the far end of the monastery, reappeared upon its roof to let down a tin on a length of string into a cistern of rain-water. Thus equipped she returned to base, cajoled her reluctant spouse to ignite a primus stove, and soon the aroma of freshly made coffee was wafted to us on the air.

Maria dilated her nostrils, sniffed the air appreciatively, and asked me what time it was. 'Midday,' I said, looking at my watch. 'We go? Perhaps to Lefteris's *Cafeneon*? For a beer?' She nodded. 'We go,' she agreed, and started to lace up her shoes. 'But I'd like to look at the chapel before we leave.'

What relics, memorabilia and mysteries lie within Saint Thomas's we shall never know for we were denied access to its interior. The rusty iron paling gate leading to a small walled courtyard was padlocked and, as we could see by looking through the arches of the colonnade, so too was the chapel door. Only the piles of empty, broken oil and wine bottles, expended stumps of candles and the faded remnants of plastic wreaths and other discarded paraphernalia of the rites of the Orthodox Church, which were heaped higgledy-piggledy against the wall, evidenced that offices were still said there; but of permanent occupation there was no sign except for a large brown rat which, standing upright with its forepaws quivering, eyed us suspiciously and beadily as it foraged in the litter.

'*Ne*,' called Mother from the picnic site, '*ine klisto* – it is closed, quite shut up. No one lives there now you understand. But come – a little coffee perhaps?' '*Efharistume*,' we said, and joined the company under the almirithra tree where bees buzzed in its branches.

'*Ne*,' she repeated as she handed around the cups, 'only once in a while, on a saint's day you understand, does a priest come to say his prayers and to light a candle.' '*Ne*,' concurred Grandma, 'but once a monk did live here with a cat. But that was long ago.' 'How long?' I asked. She shrugged her shoulders. 'Who knows?' she said, interrogatively. 'Many, many years ago. But they do say that he was struck down by the God!' And she crossed herself. '*Ne*,' endorsed Kosta, her son-in-law, offering us a biscuit, 'for being filthy.' 'Really,' we said, our prurience whetted by the prospect of being made privy to local scandal, albeit that of the distant past, and wondering about the cat. 'In what way?'

'Ah,' said Grandma emptying her cup in a single slurp and relishing the opportunity to detail the priestly enormity, 'it is, you understand, only a story but', and here she glanced about her as if to make certain that only the bees and the present company would have ears for the saga to be unfolded, 'my father – may the God rest his soul and grant him peace – was told by *his* father that this monk did something very dreadful to a young girl who daily brought him yoghurt.' She paused, allowing us to exercise our imagination and leaned towards us. 'You know what I mean?' she said, and looked at us over her spectacles. We assured her that we did. '*Endaxi*,' said Grandma, and lowered her voice dramatically.

'On the very day,' she continued, and in a style of delivery of which Henry Irving would have approved, 'indeed at the very hour that the child was due to be born to this outraged girl, the priest went out in his boat.' She paused again. 'it was', she said, entering an even lower register and sounding increasingly like Edgar Alan Poe in drag, 'a cloudless day. A *cloudless* day,' she emphasised, and once more gave us time for reflection. 'And then at the precise moment that the girl's mother placed a *keramithi* – a hot tile – upon her daughter's stomach to bring her into labour, for such was the custom, you understand, the sky grew black, the sun vanished and a jagged flash of lightning streaked from the heavens, struck the priest and', she concluded, 'he was never seen again. But,' she said, holding up her finger as if to stifle any applause, 'my father's father used to say that on certain nights the cat could still be heard calling for its master . . .'

81

There was a brief silence. Then *'Bravo Mama!'* cried Kosta and her daughter, and we all clapped. 'But do you believe such things?' 'Ah,' said Grandma, basking in her success as narrator *extraordinaire*, 'that is my secret, my children, but I know of old people who do. Many, many such people.' '*Ne*,' said Kosta, rising and dusting the seat of his trousers, 'but certainly one thing is true about the monk: *itane porno yeros* – he was a dirty old man! But then, it is well known that all priests are rams! *Ne*, they are all *kamakia* – girl-chasers.' And he laughed and grinned at his mother-in-law.

Shortly afterwards we said our thanks and good-byes and begun the return journey to Pethi, pondering as we did so that despite the lack of originality of Grandma's story, we had learned of yet another ancient custom of the Dodecanese. But, as Maria observed, were anyone to place a hot tile on her stomach during the final stages of pregnancy, it would occasion not a lightning flash but a total solar eclipse.

Very little had changed to Pethi port and its environs during our four-hour absence. The smitten couple in the beach *taverna* were still enacting their roles of Romeo and Juliet, although their drinking straws had wilted and the number of empty cans had increased, and the geriatric angler was still mesmerised by his unproductive float and line. Only the obese ginger tom had abandoned its original position. Exhausted by its extensive body-sapping lavations it was curled up, its whiskers twitching and no doubt dreaming of the pleasures of the night to come.

Further along the uphill road to Lefteris's oasis, the prickly-pear lady had rested her ample rump upon a low stone wall and was sampling the fruit which painstakingly she had pared since we last passed her. *'Herete!'* she cackled, admitting one of the succulents to her maw and proffering us another in the palm of her outstretched hand. *'Ella* – come! Take it,' she insisted as we hesitated, *'ine poli hemothes* – it is very juicy.' She was a kind soul but explicitly one whose eyesight was no longer geared for close work. Despite her efforts the offering was not as naked as a table-ready prickly-pear should be. 'Thank you,' we said, not wishing to hurt her feelings. 'We'll eat it later,' we lied, and hurried on to the *cafeneon* wondering what manner of man would greet us there.

Innocent of patrons, an air of torpor hung over Lefteris's premises. Outside, a solitary bluebottle unenthusiastically inspecting an ashtray overspilling with butt ends, provided the only life from to greet us. However, the interior to which we gained unchallenged access presented an interesting spectacle. Before us, suspended from the ceiling and slowly rotating on a fraying cord, a badly stuffed puffer fish with a dislodged glass eye and pursed lips blew us an apoplectic kiss; to our right, the jaws of two dogfish, their teeth locked in eternal grins, swung above a glass-topped bar upon which was exampled a pyramid of petrified prawns apparently engaged in a mass mating ceremony; on the wall behind them hung the print of a pipe-smoking seaman sporting a sou'wester and mutton-chop whiskers and exhorting all right-minded men to share his choice of tobacco; and on display tables throughout the room was a selection of birds, beasts and anthropoids fashioned from sea shells. Stacked crates of beer and other bottles evidenced that the establishment did provide succour for itinerant customers, but the overall impression was that of a cross between a downtown Hastings gift shop and the marine section of the Natural History Museum.

Of the mayhem of the morning there was no sign nor, until we called his name, of Lefteris. '*Oriste?*' rasped an unseen voice in unwelcoming tones from behind a closed door to the left of the bar, 'what do you want?' 'To meet you,' we said, claiming friendship with Vasili by way of introduction, and waited. A strained grunt came to us within the cubicle followed by a moment's silence broken by the clanking of a lavatory chain. '*Ena lepto,*' said the voice, 'one minute.'

Slowly the door creaked open and even more slowly Lefteris emerged from his cell. He was a slightly built, beady-eyed man in his early forties with receding black hair, long, dark sideburns, a pencil-line moustache and, like Cassius, he had a lean and hungry look. He also had very pink surrounds to his pupils.

'*Kalos*,' he said thickly, advancing towards us as though treading on cotton wool and wiping his hands on his faded denims, 'and forgive me. I was', he appraised us, clutching his head, 'at a wedding yesterday and –' He circled the air with an open palm and raised his eyebrows. '*Mana mou*,' he grated, 'such a wedding! I tell you, if the bridegroom can make love to his wife in a fortnight it will be a miracle! *Ne, ma to theo* – I am telling the truth! As for me –'

Dramatically he extended a quivering hand for Maria's inspection. '*Kitasksete!*' he said. 'Look! *Eho tremi ta treno!*' '*Ne*,' I agreed, 'you do have the shakes. But perhaps,' I said, with my tongue in my cheek, 'if you pray to Ayios Ioannis they will go. Does he not cure the ague?' '*Ne*,' volunteered Maria, equally versed in the attributes of the saints, 'or perhaps a prayer to Ayia Paraskevi who banishes headaches?' '*Ne*,' I said, 'and hangovers.'

Lefteris looked at us and allowed himself a tired smile. '*Bori*,' he said, 'perhaps. I am a believer in the powers of the saints. '*Ne*' Ayia Maura once cured my wife's third cousin of warts. But I know a better way to treat the trembles.' And he tapped his nose and moved to the bar. 'Ah,' I exclaimed as he filled a glass with raki, and remembering a phrase I had heard in Crete, '*skili poo se thangose* – of the dog that has bitten you – *vale ap'to mali tou* - hurl in some of its hair!' '*Ne*,' grinned Lefteris, 'I do not know the saying but I understand the meaning,' and drained the glass. '*Ne*,' he said, stretching forth his hand again, 'you see? It is better already. *Endaxi?*' '*Endaxi*,' we said, and obeying his instructions sat down at a table. 'Now,' said he, bringing the bottle to us and filling our glasses, 'give me news of Vasili.' We did so. 'And', we concluded, 'he told us that your food is very good.'

Lefteris looked blank. 'Food?' he repeated as if a new word had entered his vocabulary. 'Food? What type of food?' 'Well,' suggested Maria with a winning smile, '*tzatziki* for example? Or *dolmades*? Vasili told us that you had such things.' '*Ne*,'

I endorsed, 'and octopus and squid, and little fishes. We had hoped to eat with you this evening and', I added, 'to have a little something now.' 'Ah,' said Lefteris as slowly the message filtered through, 'yes, food. Indeed, food. And this evening all those things will be here I promise you. *Ne*, I will cook a big meal for you and my son Michaelis will come and play the bouzoukoi. *Ne!* We will have a little fiesta! But now,' he continued less happily and shrugging his shoulders, 'there is nothing, you understand. *Tipota!* Not even bread . . . unless . . .'

He paused as a thought struck him, then banged the table decisively. '*Ne,*' he said, 'I will go to my house and fetch some *tzatziki*. *Ne*, for the friends of Vasili I will do this thing!' And fortifying himself with another raki he rose from the table, made his way uncertainly toward the doorway, and turned to face us. 'I will', he assured us, 'be only ten minutes.'

Half an hour later he was still absent; but at two forty-five the monotony was broken. Waddling through the open door the prickly-pear lady halted before our table and exposed her ill-treated tongue. 'Ugh,' she said, and crossing to the sink, stuck it under a running tap, pronounced it better, and left. And at four o'clock we followed her example. Nor did we see Lefteris in the evening when we presented ourselves for the promised feast. The place was locked and we ate elsewhere. But we did meet him again: at church, the next morning.

It was a contrite and penitent Lefteris who approached us at the end of the service in the little church on the hill. 'What can I say?' he said kissing the hand of what must have been the oldest priest in the Orthodox Church, to whom we were talking below the outstretched wings of a plastic seagull with a broken beak which acted as a lectern. 'It was the wedding and the drink you understand. When I got to my house I could not remember why I had gone there. So I went to sleep and awoke at midnight.' And he smacked his forehead in remorse.

'Po! Po! Po!' tut-tutted the *papas* who looked like Tenniel's drawing of the White Knight, 'Such things, such things.' '*Ne,*' confessed Lefteris, '*symphono pater* – I agree. But,' he continued, addressing us directly, 'I bought two very large candles – one for each of you – and', he advised the *papas* ingratiatingly, 'I put two hundred drachmae in the plate.' *'Bravo!'* quavered the White Knight, thinking perhaps of the seagull restoration fund. *'Ine kalo!'* And invoking God to bless us all, he tottered away.

Basking is his absolution Lefteris beamed after him, then turned his attention to us. 'Tonight?' he enquired. 'You will come?' *'Ne,'* we verified, 'of course.' *'Endaxi,'* said Lefteris. And instructing us to be at the *cafeneon* at seven o'clock and swearing that if anything prevented him for being there he would stick not one but two nails through his nose, he too departed.

Lefteris honoured his promise: he was in residence that evening. So too in varying stages of euphoria was a quartet of successful hunters. Seated outside the *cafeneon* in the fading light and surrounded by piles of perforated and morose-looking pigeon and partridge they continued to exercise their marksmanship with outmoded shotguns and small-bore rifles on tin cans suspended on sticks across the road and signalled our approach with a volley. Mercifully they saw us and momentarily ceased fire. *'Ella!'* they shouted as we neared them. 'Come! You have nothing to fear unless you are partridges – or Turks!' And they laughed and encouraged us to go inside.

'Yasas!' cried Lefteris as the fusillade restarted, and greeted us with an extravagent gesture of welcome. 'Sit down,' he commanded, and pointed to a table occupied by an unsavoury-looking gentleman smelling strongly of fresh fish. 'Stavros,' he said, briskly introducing us, ' a good man. *Ne*, he has caught an octopus for us – and some *marithes*. Also my wife has made *dolmades* and *tzatziki* and I', he continued, bringing the menu to a close, 'have brought a special bottle! *Doppio krasi*,' he enlarged, 'home-made wine. And so,' he concluded with a ring of triumph and satisfied that his reputation had been restored, 'you will eat well, *ne*? But now a little raki . . .'

Half an hour later with the air thick with the smell of

frying fish we did justice to all that was put before us. So too did Smelly Stavros, Lefteris's thirteen-year-old son Michaelis, who arrived and played the bouzoukoi between mouthfuls, and so too did the hunters who, denied by darkness from further target practice, joined us at the table together with their spoils. It was a happy if odoriferous gathering. Softened by music and wine we laughed and sang, and as if by magic more bottles appeared. And so, in the midst of our revels did a flustered Nikos Pipsos.

'Ah,' he exclaimed after greetings had been exchanged and he had taken possession of a glass and swiftly lowered its level, 'I have been looking for you everywhere. *Ne*, I have most important news for you – by telephone from Zagorianos in Rhodes. *Ne!* About the Smarlwad!' I looked puzzled. 'Small World,' interpreted Maria. '*Ne*,' said Pipsos, a little irritably, 'the Smarlwad boat.'

'The Smarlwad boat?' said Smelly Stavros, pricking up his ears, 'I know the Smarlwad boat. O Yannis from Lindos who has a way with women and an ulcer, he brings it here often, full of white English people. *Ne*, they go to Panormitis to see the monastery and the statue of the abbot whom the Germans shot. Have you been there?' he inquired of us. We shook our heads. 'Ah,' said Stavros spearing the remaining *marithes*, 'you should. *Ne*, go there tomorrow.' Impatient of these diversions Pipsos drummed on the table. '*Oche*,' he said, 'you will not go there tomorrow. Nor will the Smarlwad. And do you know why?' he asked rhetorically. 'Because', he continued dramatically, 'the Smarlwad has a hole in it – indeed a very, very large hole.'

There was a short silence. Then:

'*Oche!*' said Lefteris incredulously.

'*Ne!*' said Nikos emphatically; and elaborated.

The story unfolded to a rapt audience hungry for detail was a convoluted one, even when précised.

Captain Yannis, he advised us, more than usually aggravated by his ulcer, had gone to hospital for medical attention having recommended to the owners of the vessel that a close relative of his should be given temporary command of it. They could, he had assured his employers, have perfect confidence in the gentleman who was unulcerated, responsible and a demon navigator to boot. Unfortunately for the company, its clientele and good family relations, within two days the close relative had exposed the danger of nepotism and a hitherto undisclosed condition of myopia by steering his craft unerringly on to some large rocks in the Cyclades, and there it remained. No one, continued Nikos, was very pleased, particularly Captain Yannis who, he understood, when advised by this maritime misadventure had developed a second ulcer. But no matter. As a result of the debacle the company had had to mollify twenty-two disgruntled, shocked and sea-soaked passengers, reschedule their cruising programme and charter a new boat called the *Ismeni* under the command of a captain whose name escaped him. This, he informed us, would be waiting our arrival at Mandraki harbour in Rhodes on the morrow to transport us to other islands, the exact location of which he was in ignorance. 'And that,' concluded Nikos Pipsos refreshing himself with more raki, 'is what Yiorgo Zagorianos has told me. That is the message given to him by telephone from your friend Colin in London.'

'Po! Po! Po!' said Smelly Stavros shaking his head as the saga finished. 'As my father told me, nothing good comes out of the Cyclades – only wind.' '*Ne*,' agreed Lefteris in unison with the hunters, 'and wrecks.' And replenishing their glasses they held a lengthy post-mortem on the catastrophe and fell to speculating on the present state of Captain Yannis' ulcer.

As we were to discover, thanks to our own move-ments and the multifarious shortcomings of the Greek telecommunications system, the news of the incident had been slow in reaching us. Moreover, the unexpurgated version related by Nikos had contained a number of minor but actionable inaccuracies concerning the cause of Captain Yannis' first ulcer; but the facts remained. Our stay in Simi was to be curtailed, Pipsos would ensure that we caught the Monday afternoon ferry, and that on disembarking we would be met by a representative of the lamented *Small World's* crew and conducted to the *Ismeni*.

'*Thenbirazi*,' said Lefteris sorrowfully, as later we expressed our regret and prepared to take our leave. 'Never mind,' said he, presenting us with a bag of figs stuffed with almonds and sesame seeds, 'you must come back'. '*Ne*,' echoed Smelly Stavros and the hunters, 'return and shoot with us in the hills. Had you not been leaving tomorrow we would have given you a *perthica* – a partridge; but as it is it might go bad.' And they embraced us and wished us farewell.

So did the Marias the following afternoon. 'For the voyage,' said Maria the elder, thrusting a bag of cooked beans to to my Maria. 'One never knows these days.' '*Ne*,' said her sister, crossing herself and giving me a bunch of basil, 'one never knows.' And they waved to us as a tardy Nikos Pipsos drove us away to catch the ferry in the very nick of time.

'*Ella!*' screamed Vasili as our baggage was hurled aboard, 'we go, yes?' '*Ne*,' we cried, 'we go!' And quickly hugging Nikos Pipsos and thanking him for his kindness, we staggered aboard the SS *Lindos*. '*Andio!*' we shouted as we pulled away from the quay. '*Andio! Andio! Andio!*'

6

Ismeni Ahoy!

Without distractions such as the Moosehead Beer Trio who, we conjectured, were still engrossed in tweaking sea-urchin spines from the soles of their feet, the return journey to Rhodes could have been boring. As it was, thanks to the narrative and histrionic skills of Captain Vasili, it was merely tedious.

Captain Vasili, it transpired, knew all about Captain Yannis' brother-in-law's contretemps in the Cyclades. Indeed, before we had progressed less than three **leagues** from Simi, we had been appraised not only of the navigational imperfections of that unfortunate but of the many other peccadilloes of his entire clan – and in every particular. Much of the imparted intelligence was, we suspected, the product of his imagination but it was a fascinating chronicle and we absorbed every salacious detail of it. However, with regard to news of the impending captaincy of the *Ismeni*, Vasili was less well informed. Much, he deliberated between sips of his favourite prophylactic, could depend upon the vessel's owner, one Takis, a man of some influence and fortune. It was he, he mused, who would have the casting vote between, he believed, a Mister Manolis and a Mister Satiris, both of Rhodes town, but doubtless by the time we made port the matter would have been resolved. Conversely, his knowledge of the credentials and origins of the remainder of the *Ismeni's* crew was very full.

There was, he advised us, as we neared the end of the journey and approached the twin-pillared bronze antelopes marking the entrance to the anchorage with the fort of Saint Nicholas to its left, a complement of six. A young Welshman and an Asian named Ram Singh who were employed as deck hands; three nubile girls who catered for the creature comforts of the passengers; and a purser who, he opined, like all of that calling, screwed the women, made a lot of money and did little work. Of the three hostesses he spoke with warmth and kindness. The senior one was a willowly Australian and the second a diminutive Scot. But it was the third member who had imposed herself indelibly on his memory.

'*Mana mou* Yanni,' he sighed, wide-eyed with remembrance and balancing imaginary spheres in either hand and weighing them at chest-level, 'what a woman! Po! Po! Po! *Ne* Yanni, *ehi visia san karpoosia* Yanni – she has tits like water-melons! *Ne ine sosta* – it is true! *Big* water-melons. And,' he continued, careering further down the Gadarine slope of indelicacy and putting me even more in mind of the Song of Solomon, '*ti popos* – what a bottom! I tell you, Yanni, when you see her you will not want to eat meat for a year!' 'Really?' said Maria, turning to me with the aplomb of a nursing sister who has seen everything, and not in the least embarrassed by Vasili's anatomical inventory nor his allegorical touches, 'then while you go vegetarian, I'll look for the purser.'

Vasili roared with laughter. '*Oche!*' he said, as close upon six o'clock his second-in-command navigated the ferry to its berth. '*Ine ta skoopedia* – he is rubbish!' And he laughed again loudly and pointed downward to the quayside. '*Kitakste!*' he said. 'Look! That is the Stallion of the Sea!'

We followed his finger and found its target. It was a small, unremarkable man possessed of thinning black hair, stone-coloured slacks and a dun-checked shirt marked out like graph paper. Even his spectacles were unframed. Through them, unenthusiastically, he scanned the now disembarking passengers. We waited until all but a few had left the ship and then, after saying our farewells, followed the remainder ashore and confronted him.

'Good evening,' I said brightly, planting my suitcase at his feet while Maria did likewise with hers. 'I believe you're from the *Ismeni*.' Disbelievingly the Stallion of the Sea stared hard at our disreputable and tattered baggage, wrinkled his nose at it and then directed his gaze towards me, his face a mask of indifference and boredom. 'Ah,' he said colourlessly, offering us each in turn a limp hand and then withdrawing it with indecent haste as if regretting the gesture, 'you must be the Egbons.' 'Well,' I said, lightly brushing the error aside, 'if we must we must but actually we're the Ebdons. Ha! Ha!'

The badinage was ill-received. 'I'm sorry,' he said coldly, 'it must have been the telex. Mistakes, you understand, do happen.' His voice was tenor, his delivery staccato, and his vowels pinched. 'However,' he continued with vibrant insincerity, 'I'm pleased to meet you.' He cleared his throat. 'And now,' he commanded, 'follow me.' And allowing Maria to carry her bag he set off at a brisk pace along the line of anchored boats. Fourteen vessels down the row he halted before the gangway of the *Ismeni* and paused at its foot. 'And this', said he, allowing himself a wintry smile, 'is your home for the next two weeks. Welcome aboard!' he said, and precariously led the way up the rope-railed swaying steps and on to the deck.

The *Ismeni* was an elegant sixty-foot tops'l schooner with beautiful lines. She had a white hull inset with seven portholes a side, a teak superstructure enclosing the living-quarters and a sun-deck atop of it. Aft of that was the bridge and below it the ship's galley. And it was before that that we were brought to a stop. Through its open door wafted the smell of cordon bleu exotica on the threshold of fruition and from within, and in answer to the Stallion's call, came a tall, attractive, golden-tanned, blonde-headed girl perspiring freely and smiling broadly.

'Hi there!' she twanged in the unmistakable accents of New South Wales. 'Good to see you! I'm Sophie. and that', said she, pointing through the cooking haze to a swim-suited companion in the process of offering a tray of delicacies to a Calor gas stove, 'is Bettina. Betts,' she screamed, 'come and meet the folks!' 'Hello!' said Betts heartily, setting down the load of goodies and spilling out of her magenta bikini as she advanced towards us, 'jolly nice to see you.' As we shook hands I wondered if she had played hockey for Roedean but instinctively I knew that she was Vasili's dream girl and I marvelled at Mother Nature's ability to pour so much of her handiwork into one young woman.

'So there we are,' beamed Sophie. 'Now you've only got to meet Ian and Izzie but they're ashore buying booze for tonight's Welcome Aboard Party, and little Ram Singh's unblocking a loo; but they'll be around later. Anyhow,' she said, wiping her brow on a convenient dishcloth, 'come on, I'll show you below to your cabin.' She picked up Maria's bag and turned to the Stallion of the Sea who was still in attendance. 'OK?' she enquired of him, crisply and with little warmth. 'OK by you?' 'Of course,' he said, 'I have things to do,' and nodding to us made his way quickly down the deck, turned inboard and disappeared. Sophie eyed his departure and nudged Maria. 'Watch him,' she advised, 'he's a shit – got more hands than a bloody octopus. Anyway, follow me . . .'

The living-quarters through which she took us were pleasantly, even delicately, furnished. For'ard was a small, well-equipped bar faced with mahogany strips; to port and starboard were floral-curtained, rounded rectangular windows and below them beige moquette-covered comfortable bench seats were separated by tables with imitation wood-grained formica tops. Seated around one of them, in line with one of two spiral staircases leading to what euphemistically were called cabins, was a trio of Greeks. All were peering at the table top as if examining it for flaws; and all exuded an aura of tension.

'Conclave,' muttered Sophie as we passed them unnoticed and descended into the ship's bowels. 'They're deciding who's going to steer us onto the next bloody rocks. I'll introduce you when we come up.'

Below, for'ard and to starboard we inspected our quarters. Had we been pigmies we would have rejoiced in their roominess. As it was we looked at the stunted bunks with some concern. 'Never mind,' giggled Sophie sensing our lack of euphoria. 'Just cut off your feet, bend double and pretend you're a U-boat captain.' She laughed uproariously at her sally and slapped me on the back. 'But,' she added, abandoning her levity and severely wagging a finger at both of us, 'never, *ever* put anything down the whatsit that you shouldn't. Know what I mean?' We assured her that we did. 'Good oh,' said she, smiling again. 'Well that's about it. Now let's go aloft and meet the mafiosi.'

Backward, bent, and leading the way, I exited from the nautical rabbit hutch but abruptly came to a halt as my backside made contact with something soft. It was a curious sensation. Momentarily I paused, turned around with difficulty, and found that my bottom gently had kissed that of an advancing septuagenarian lady who had emerged from her cabin in similar style.

'Ah-ha-ha!' exclaimed the grey-haired and bespectacled aged one clasping her rear with one hand and a pigskin-covered hip flask with the other. 'So sorry! Awfully cramped down here, don't you think?' 'Yes,' we said, 'awfully,' and followed Sophie down the narrow corridor separating the cabins.

'Great old lady that,' said Sophie cocking her thumb backward as we progressed. 'Close on eighty, would you believe? Flew in yesterday with the others, dumped her bags, changed, dived into the 'ogwash like there was no tomorrow, had a couple of whiskies and then went out on the town with her Pentax. Yeah. Told me she'd sold an antique vee-o-lin cheller to pay for the hols and was going to get honked every day on the proceeds. Yeah! Great sport.' 'Yes,' we said, looking over our shoulders to see the Great Sport addressing herself to her flask and then waving it at us in salutation, 'she certainly seems to be.' 'Yeah,' repeated Sophie as we spiralled upward again, 'too right.'

As when we had passed them on our way below, the Greek trio seated at their table in the living-quarters made an unhappy threesome. One, a moustached and bad-tempered looking man in his early thirties with dark smouldering eyes and a prematurely receding hairline, tapped impatiently upon the table; the second, in his mid-twenties, gave the impression

'Ah-ha-ha!'

that the worst was about to happen; while the third, in his late forties and also clean-shaven, left us in no doubt that it had. Hollow-eyed and with sunken cheeks untouched by a razor for several days, he appeared to have been exhumed: and quite recently. All in all they made a lugubrious gathering and one not improved by the addition of the Stallion of the Sea who had joined them during our absence below.

'Ah,' said that gentleman, reluctantly raising himself from his seat by a centimetre in deference to Maria as Sophie steered us toward the ensemble, 'so we meet again.' Unenthusiastically he introduced us by name: to Takis the ship's owner and finger-tapper who spoke good English; to the cadaverous Captain Manoli, who was similarly talented having acquired a travesty of our language whilst serving in an American tanker in the Gulf; and to the younger captain, Sotiris. Denied of even a working knowledge of a lingua franca and at first acquaintance seemingly not particularly articulate in his own tongue, understandably the last-named was comparatively silent; but he had an engaging smile. All wished us well, politely congratulated us on our Greek and then, lighting fresh cigarettes, peered at the table again.

'Well,' said Sophie brightly, 'which one of these jokers is going to shipwreck us, eh?' The Stallion looked at her balefully. 'They both are,' he said, 'and Mr Takis is coming with us as well. There have been', he enlarged wearily, 'certain differences of opinion and it seemed better that way.' 'Yes,' said Takis taking over the conversational helm 'much better.' He spoke quickly, emphatically, and in short bursts. 'My ship, my lovely ship, she is new – I do not want happenings with her. Not like Smarlwad. I want, how to say, to keep the eye on her. You understand. Yes? Good! Very good. That is why I come.'

Nervously he drummed afresh on the table, inhaled on his cigarette and noisily ejected a thin stream of smoke. 'Also,' he continued, 'there was a problem. A big problem.' He inhaled again. 'Captain Yannis of Smarlwad wishes Sotiris to be captain of my lovely ship. OK! I agree! He is a very good boy, I like him very very much, but', he said stubbing his finger thrice and imperiously upon the table, 'for my opinion my friend Manolis has a better knowledge of the coastlines of the islands we shall visit. I do not want', he reiterated, 'another bam-bam on the rocks. Correct?' he inquired of Manolis. 'That is so – you know the charts?' 'Correct,' agreed Manolis sepulchrally, 'like the back of my arse. Also,' he added, glancing at Sotiris but without malice, 'this one is a bit of a dum-dum.'

Uncomprehending of the slur on his intellectual rating, Sotiris smiled at him bovinely and said nothing. 'Ha! Ha!' said Takis, benevolently patting him on the face. 'That is so. Completely. *But*,' he concluded with the air of a Daniel come to judgement, 'because we shall be visiting Kusadasi where Manolis was imprisoned by the Turks,' and here he spat into the ashtray, 'Sotiris will be coming as second captain in case something happens. We cannot,' he finalised, 'be too careful.' 'Indeed,' said the Stallion, removing his glasses and polishing them and possibly thinking of the misadventures of the *Small World*, 'indeed we can't.' He looked very tired and suddenly I felt sorry for him. It would, I mused, be some days before he was at stud again.

He rose apologetically from the table. 'So that's the form,' he said. 'And now if you'll excuse me, I have things to do.' He glanced at his digital watch. 'See you,' he said, smiling wanly, 'in half an hour – at the briefing; and then at the party. *Argotera*', he said, for the benefit of Sotiris, 'later.'

'My oath!' muttered Sophie as we left them. '*Three* bloody captains! This, folks, is going to be fun. See you in church . . .'

The briefing held in the living-quarters was reminiscent of Assembly on the first day of term in Big School. Seated in duos, trios and quartets around the table with the occasional singletons self-consciously occupying solitary positions, the mostly middle-aged new boys and girls, all strangers one to the other save for the intimacy of their immediate companions, expectantly looked aft awaiting the entrance of the Headmaster and his staff, and his address. Conversation was desultory and stilted.

'When, I wonder', plaintively inquired a sixty-year-old woman with a large lump on her forehead and a ginny voice, who was in tandem with an elderly gentleman sporting a tortoise hat and a Wellington cravat, 'will the bar open?' 'Soon I hope,' responded an isolated contemporary with bulging eyes, 'very soon.' Seated in a corner the Great Sport laughed, winked at her nearest neighbour and tapped the handbag meaningfully. 'No problem,' she said happily. 'Like a good boy scout I'm always prepared, don't you know! Ha! Ha!' Eyes turned toward her in disapproving silence. Then:

'I've brought me own lilo and a hand pump,' said a very white fat man in the deep ponderous accents of Humberside, 'so I can blow it up,' he explained. 'Really?' said the Lady with the Lump condescendingly and confirming Bernard Shaw's judgement that it is impossible for one Englishman to open his mouth without making another of his countrymen despise him, 'how quaint. What's your name?' The bleached one looked at her shyly. 'Walter,' he said, slowly splitting the word into two syllables, 'but folk call me Wally.' 'Ha! Ha!' exclaimed the Lady with the Lump, and dug the Wellingtonian in his midriff. 'I say, did you hear that? We've got a Wally on board!' 'What's that?' quavered her husband fingering a grizzled walrus moustache and peering uninterestedly at his spouse through granny glasses. 'What d'ye say?' His wife sucked her teeth impatiently. 'I said –' she broke off as the Stallion of the Sea made his entrance together with his acolytes. 'Never mind,' she snapped crossly. 'Shh!'

To his credit the *deus ex machina* of the ship had gone to some trouble to dispel the hostile aura which previously he had dispensed. Not only was he wearing a freshly laundered shirt freely decorated with white anchors and sea-horses disporting themselves on a maroon background, and his best aftershave lotion, but he had dug deep into the hidden depths of his alter ego and now emanated a hitherto undisclosed professional bonhomie.

'Ladies and gentlemen,' he said, smiling through his teeth and exuding spurious goodwill, 'officially may we welcome

98

you aboard the *Ismeni*.' He gestured toward his staff of five and a scattered burst of applause acted as a breakwater before his next utterance. 'Thank you, thank you,' he acknowledged in the best David Frost style and smoothing a hand over his newly oiled hair, 'and thank *you*. Now,' he continued 'most of you have met Sophie and Bettina, and of course' he added 'you all know me.' His eyes scanned the passengers, in a vain hope of evidence of unattached female talent under forty, and clouded visibly when they drew a blank. 'However,' he went on, admirably hiding his disappointment, 'you have not yet met Izzie; or Ian.'

'Izzie,' he advised us, moving toward an attractive brunette who was holding hands with a young, fair-haired Welshman, 'when not preoccupied with Ian, also cooks and makes your beds and Ian, when not otherwise engaged with Izzie, is responsible for the general maintenance of the ship. You know what I mean,' he said.

His innuendoes received a mixed reception from the assembled and particularly from the nominated sinners who, smiling obediently, sank further into their seats. 'Nor', he pursued, 'have you come across the ship's mascot and general factotum, Ram Singh.' Rising, and delicately placing his fingertips together, the last named, an undernourished Asian with hugely prominent white teeth displayed in a perpetual grin, looked upon the company, said 'Very good, isn't it?' and sat down again to enthusiastic and prolonged clapping, proving beyond doubt that the British, publicly, will always show their support for those who they consider to be under-dogs, and coloured ones to boot.

Indulgently the Stallion smiled upon us. 'And lastly but by no means least', he concluded, completing the introduction to his *dramatis personae* and discouraging Ram Singh from taking an encore in answer to his audience's request for one, 'is Mr Takis, owner of the good ship *Ismeni* and our two captains, Messrs Sotiris and Manolis.' Of the three men to whom he waved in salutation and encouragement only Manolis failed to respond. Seated opposite us at our table he focused his gaze upon its surface, his deep-set eyes seemingly looking at everything except that which was around him while the smoke from his wasting cigarette curled through his nicotine-stained fingers. Maria put out her hand and let it rest lightly on the back of his. *'Ti simveni?'* she asked softly – 'What's the matter?' Slowly Manolis met her eyes. *'Tipota,'* he said – 'nothing; but thank you for asking.'

'And now,' said the Stallion, 'some facts and figures for all of us. Firstly, meals.' 'Ah!' said a pasty-faced, paunchy father and son in chorus from behind us. 'Yes, meals!' 'Breakfast', advised the Stallion, 'will be continental in style, in other words, bags of honey or jam, fresh warm bread, tea or coffee, all served between eight and nine o'clock. And,' he warned us, 'if you don't like *cold* bread, get up early.' 'Ah,' said the porcine couple, 'ah.'

'Luncheon', continued the Stallion, 'will be a running buffet with unlimited wine at one o'clock, and dinner, a sit-down affair – again with unlimited wine – will be at seven thirty.' There was a general murmur of approval. 'What about tea?' inquired Big and Little Pig Robinson to our rear, 'do we get tea?' The Stallion looked at them disparagingly. 'Tea,' he confirmed, 'for those who wish it, will be available at four o'clock, and the bar', he added, 'will open daily from ten thirty.' Again there was a buzz of appreciation. 'Good oh!' said the matron with the bulging eyes. 'I'll be there!' '*And* me!' echoed the Lady with the Lump. 'Won't we?' she inquired of the Wellingtonian, 'won't we just!' 'What's that?' he said. 'What d'ye say?' . . .

'And now', said the Stallion, reasserting his authority as the susurration died down, 'to more mundane matters.' He cleared his throat. 'Lavatories,' he said, 'lavatories;' and then elaborated in detail on that of which we had been apprised by Sophie. To the innocent his news was indelicate if not downright unpleasant and there was a noticeable sigh of relief when he turned our attention to other less basic matters of hygiene, namely hairdriers.

'Ladies,' said the Stallion ingratiatingly, 'as you all know,

the salt air plays havoc with the hair and therefore', he coun-
selled, 'it is essential that daily you keep your splendid locks
in good order. Ha! Ha! And so,' he indicated, 'a point for
hairdriers can be found behind the bar. Just plug in, ladies,
and you'll be OK. *Endaxi?*' he inquired presuming that the
assembled were cognisant of that one Greek word, *endaxi*.
'*Endaxi*,' chorused the ladies, '*endaxi!*' 'No trouble,' said the
Great Sport from the corner of the room and possessed of a
grey Eton crop. 'I wear a wig in the evening.'

'That's all very well,' said the Wellingtonian rising and
removing his hat to reveal a bald head and presenting us
with a remarkable facsimile of an upstage Alf Garnett,
'but what about mains razors?' The Stallion looked blank.
'Mains razors?' he enquired, 'mains razors?' 'Yes,' said the
Wellingtonian, 'mains razors.'

'What about mains razors?'

'Well, I have one.'

'Yes?'

'Not a battery you understand, but a mains razor.'

'Yes, yes.'

'One plugs it in.'

'One would.'

'Precisely. And one switches on.'

'Exactly.'

'But where?'

'What?'

'Where does one plug in and switch on?' asked the
Wellingtonian, showing signs of irritability, '*where?*' 'In the
same place as the hairdrier,' said the Stallion also exhibiting
symptoms of stress. 'Well, why the devil didn't you say so
in the first place?' wheezed the Wellingtonian and sat down.
'Dammed idiot,' he muttered breathing heavily. 'Bloody fool.
Grammar school, I shouldn't wonder.' The Stallion glared at
him. 'King's Canterbury actually,' he said, and recovered his
composure with difficulty. 'But now, ladies and gentlemen,'
he concluded glossing over what had promised to be an unfortunate domestic scene and bringing the seminar to a close, 'it

only remains for me to tell you that tomorrow morning we'll
be sailing to Panormitis in Simi and that in half an hour we'll
have the pleasure of meeting you all again at the Eve of
Sailing Party here. But for the moment, if you'll excuse me,
I have things to do.'

Accompanied by the Lady with the Lump, the Wellingtonian rose slowly from his seat and joined the others on
their way down to their cabins to prepare for the bacchanal to
come; but from that time on he became known to the entire
ship's company as 'Mains Razor' – even to Manolis.

'See you later?' we asked him as we made to leave. 'At
the party?' Up went his eyebrows in the unspoken negative.
'Tomorrow,' he said. 'I am not in the mood for parties.' And
lighting a fresh cigarette from the stub of the previous one,
he left the ship with the gait of a man upon whose shoulders
rested all the cares of the world. 'And frankly,' said Maria as
we watched him go, 'neither am I.' 'Nor me,' I said, rubbing
my chin, 'but *noblesse oblige* I suppose. Anyway, come on –
I need a shave.'

By the time we presented ourselves at eight fifteen the party
was already well under way. Second by second the warm air
thickened with tobacco smoke and the smells of unguents and
underarm deodorants, and minute by minute the decibel level
increased as, in the accepted style of all cocktail parties anywhere, everyone talked at the tops of their voices, and nobody
said very much. 'How-do-you-dos' and Christian names were
bellowed and exchanged, places of origin disclosed and discreet
probes made as to backgrounds and occupations by all except
Big and Little Pig Robinson. Too preoccupied for small talk
of any kind, like a pair of demented truffle hounds they thrust
and jostled through the throng in search of trays of eatables,
and demolished all that came in their path with a frightening
single-mindedness and turn of speed.

'My God!' cried the Great Sport, similarly hypnotised by
the reapers' progress and politely elbowing her way toward us
beaming and now bewigged in a blue-grey creation. 'Puts one
in mind of vacuum cleaners don't you think? Still, takes all

sorts doesn't it?' 'Certainly does,' shrilled a youngish blonde woman unwisely robed in a form-hugging off-the-shoulder little number in black jersey silk, who we later discovered sold crystallized fruit in Fortnum and Mason's, 'it certainly does! My name's Cynthia,' she screamed; 'and yours?' We enlightened her. '*Super*,' she said, approaching top C, 'but what do you *do*?' Maria volunteered her profession and I mine. 'I broadcast,' I yelled. 'Oh really?' she trumpeted, 'On *what*?' 'Well,' I boomed back, my ego dented by her admission of non-recognition, 'I've a programme on B.B.C Radio 4 called –

'Yes!' screeched a woman's voice close at hand, whose name I learnt was Patience but who unlike her poetic counterpart had, I conjectured, never smiled at anything, let alone grief. 'You do! You certainly do! The wireless! Yes! Yes,' she went on aggressively waving an impaled gherkin under my nose and stridently addressing all within earshot, ' he uses pieces from BBC recordings – *innocent* things people have said in interviews – and then makes fun of them. Yes, that's what he does! Don't you?' she accused in a high vibrato. 'Don't you? And *that* I can tell you', she complained to an ever-growing audience who, arrested by her rhetoric had abandoned their own conversations and tuned in to our wavelength, 'is what he'll do here – won't you? Yes,' she continued in rising cadence, 'that's what he'll do! He'll listen to everything! Everything we say, and then *use* it!' The gherkin all but entered my left nostril. 'Admit it!' she screamed, approaching the threshold of hysteria, her free hand tightening upon her chain-mail handbag, 'admit it!'

For the first and only time in my life, deliberately I was rude to a woman. 'Madam,' I said, 'what makes you think that anything you might say will be of the slightest interest to me – or to anybody?'

The gherkin trembled uncontrollably upon its stick and fell off. 'Oh!' she gasped, and sat down abruptly upon a tray of assorted canapés. 'Oh!' she reiterated, mercifully oblivious of her cushion. 'How dare you! I've never, never been spoken to like that before – never!' 'Well,' said Walter, his thoughts momentarily diverted from his pump and lilo and breaking the ensuing silence, 'she'll not be able to say that again.' 'No,' endorsed the Great Sport draining her glass and commanding a refill as Patience, assisted by Bettina and Sophie, departed in disarray with a squashed *bonne bouche* still attached to her floral-patterned rear, 'and personally I think you're jolly amusin' don't you know.' I smiled gratefully. 'Thank you,' I said. 'At least I try not to do any actual harm.' But we left shortly after the incident and went ashore.

In the heart of the old city of Rhodes in a dingy *taverna* hidden in a side street close to Saint Catherine's Gate and far away from the tourist track, we had a long and leisurely meal. Noisily and like hungry thrushes we sucked *kochlios* – those brown humbug-coloured little snails marinated in garlic and tomato sauce – from their shells and then enjoyed the main meal of *calamarakia* cooked in wine, sweet fresh mullet, and two bottles of retsina. Then, happy, replete and hand in hand, we made our way back through the medieval streets of Rhodes.

At half past midnight the long Street of the Knights was empty and there in the stillness of the small hours I swore I could hear their horses' hooves and the clank of steel as they clattered over the cobbles on their way to the castle. And I heard voices murmuring to me from the shadows in the tongues of the Knights of St John: from the Auvergne and Provence, Italy and France, and from Germany, England and Spain. The street was filled with the ghosts of six hundred years ago and we whispered one to the other as if we were in church, and then kept silence.

With our arms around each other's waists we reached Mandraki harbour, walked past the festoons of fairy lights still glowing fitfully in loops above the closing restaurants with their piled and upturned chairs outside them, watched the posses of marauding cats searching for forgotten fish heads in the light of the moon, and so past the lines of anchored boats with their halyards tinkling like Japanese wind chimes in the gentle breeze, and back to the *Ismeni*.

'Hi!' called Sophie as we stepped across the threshold from the deck and into the living-quarters where she and her companions were sprawled around a table. 'Come on over and meet Izzie and Ian and Ram Singh. We're just putting our feet up after the booze-up. Strewth,' she said, rubbing the back of her hand across her forehead, 'those gannets cleared the flaming decks! What'll you have? Wine?' We nodded. 'Good oh,' she said. 'Betts, get a couple of glasses, there's a love. You having another?' she inquired of Ian as Bettina made her way to the galley. 'One for the bunk?' 'Why not?' said Ian in a mild Carmarthanshire accent and caressing Izzie's thigh in mid-sentence. 'And one for Izzie while you're about it. But not for Ram Singh,' he said, 'he's only drinking Coke, aren't you boyo?' 'Oh yes please,' said Ram Singh wagging his head and grinning from ear to ear. 'Only Coke I am drinking because of religion isn't it?' 'Like hell it is!' snorted Ian. 'I can smell the rum from here you bloody liar!' 'Ha! Ha! Ha!' said Ram Singh, repeating his impression of a metronome and grinning even more broadly. 'Yes, I am one bloody lying wog isn't it? Ha! Ha!' He sipped from his glass with evident enjoyment. 'Oh yes,' he said replacing it upon the table, 'same same Coke. Cheery bung old fellow,' he proclaimed, and raised it again.

Despite the overtone of pidgin it came as no surprise to us to learn that Ram Singh had acquired his English whilst serving as a bearer in the Bombay Yacht Club. As to why he had relinquished that prestigious post we were never enlightened. Nor did we ask. It is one of the unwritten rules of the sea that one does not inquire into the reasons why some temporary seamen take to the deep, and we honoured it.

'Well here's to you both,' toasted Sophie taking two long glasses from the returning Bettina and filling them. 'Have fun. But jeeze – that was quite a production number earlier on, wasn't it? My oath, she loathes your guts!' 'Golly, yes,' said Bettina topping up her own tumbler. 'Frightful old bat. Threw the most awful wobbly in her cabin afterwards – gosh she did. Said she wanted to go home and all that sort of thing.' 'Not to worry,' said Sophie, 'there's one on every cruise isn't there?' 'Um,' agreed Izzie, gently steering Ian's hand away from what then she considered was forbidden territory, 'menopausal I reckon.' 'That's right,' said Ian undeterred by her gesture and continuing on course as if guided by radar. 'Remember Porthole Pam? Swore a rat with a straw hat on was looking at her through the window. *And* smoking a cigar too he was she said. Diw, Diw,' he sighed as the horrid memories came flooding back. 'Doolally she was in my opinion.' 'Oh-my-God-yes,' said Ram Singh, 'Also she was after my body isn't it?' 'Yeah,' said Ian unkindly, 'like I said boy, she was round the twist.' And they all laughed and fell about, including little Ram Singh. 'Still,' said Sophie when the laughter stopped, 'we've a fair variety aboard this time when you think about it.'

We looked at her quizzically. 'Oh yes,' she said, addressing me, 'apart from your one-woman fan club we've got a beetle expert from the British Museum, but she's OK, a couple from Lancashire who've not stopped bickering since they arrived, and a lady with a rumbling tum – allergic to herbs, she is. Yeah, we've got to make up a separate platter for her every bloody day. Yeah,' she repeated, 'add that lot to Walter the Wally, Mains Razor and the two hoovering gents and I reckon we're in for a ball, don't you folks?' She laughed uproariously and started to collect the empties as the company broke up. 'Incidently,' I asked as she stacked the glasses, 'where's you-know-who?' Sophie paused in her labours and frowned. 'Himself?' she said. 'Dunno. But in his words, I expect he's got things to do. Mind you', she added running a finger from right to left under her nose, 'with this load of talent he'll have his work cut out, my word he will.' And bearing the tray away she made toward the galley with Bettina. 'Goodnight,' they called, 'sleep tight.'

I did not sleep tight. Like Shakespeare's wretched Clarence in *Richard III* before his unfortunate encounter with the butt of Malmsey, my dreams were full of fearful shapes and fantasies. Like Patience . . . and Porthole Pam . . .

7

Able and Other Seamen

At 10 o'clock the following morning we slipped our moorings, and with three blasts on the ship's siren and a line of smalls fluttering in competition with the Greek flag we inched our way backward through the green water and pulled away from the ranks of anchored craft. Five minutes on and accompanied by an ominous rattling sound from somewhere aft and a stream of blasphemy from Ian who was looking over the side, we came to an abrupt halt as we fouled an anchor chain. 'Oh-my-God,' said little Ram Singh who was also in attendance, 'we-have-been-buggered-up-isn't-it?' And from the wheelhouse came the cry of a soul in anguish.

Anticipating that his worst fears had been realised, Takis flew down the steps as if pursued by demons, elbowed Ram Singh and Ian out of his way and peered over the stern to see what had happened to his pride and joy. 'Ahh!' he screamed, smacking his forehead with his hand and semaphoring to his co-captains on the bridge. 'You fools, you fools! What have you done?' *Tipota*,' shouted Sotiris, similarly animated, 'nothing. It is only a small thing – no problem. We move a little to port!' '*Oche!*' bellowed Manolis, 'to starboard I think!' 'No! No!' yelled Takis, perspiring freely. 'We go forward again, and then backward! Oh my boat, my lovely boat!' 'My God!' cried the Great Sport who with the entire ship's complement had lined the deck to watch the performance. 'Hope we can all swim, what? Ha! Ha!' Next to her the lady reported to be allergic to herbs turned a shade paler, inhaled sharply and went inside. So too did Patience. The Great Sport watched their departure in silence and then turned to us. 'No sense of fun those two, don't you know. Care for a snort?'

To the relief of everyone, and thanks to the efforts of Ram Singh and Ian who freed us from the underwater encumbrance by brute force and a grappling hook, we sailed for our first destination; but the ensuing post-mortem of the incident by the Captains Courageous which clearly could be heard on deck did little to reassure us that the triumvirate was the best that money could buy. Nor did the episode do anything to lift the clouds of melancholia which continued to hover about Manolis's head.

Three miles' sail away from the port of Panormitis in the south of Simi, we found him leaning over the stern rail, staring at the *Ismeni's* wake and clasping a bunch of fading *vasilico* and two jaded roses tied together with string. From the bridge came the sound of bouzoukoi music from Athens transmitted over the ship's radio, but he neither heard nor saw anything. Nor immediately did he acknowledge our presence when we joined him but continued to gaze into the water.

'*Pos pais?*' asked Maria, touching him on the shoulder. 'How goes it?' He shrugged his shoulders and sighed. '*Etsiketsi,*' he said, 'so so.' Then, raising the spray of flowers and herbs to his lips he kissed it, crossed himself three times, and tossed it into the blue and white foam. Uncomprehendingly we watched the posy bob and float away.

There was a long silence and then at last Manolis spoke. 'For the Ayios Michaelis,' he said, 'the Panormitis. Always one sends a gift to the Blessed One at his monastery, that is the custom – to renew our vows to him and the Christian faith. And next month, Yanni, thousands from all over the Dodecanese, from Rhodes and Kassos, Kalymnos and Nisyros, all will strew the sea with their presents. *Ne*, on November the eighth that will happen, for that is the day of his *panegiris*, his religious celebration. And I tell you something, Yanni,' and he waved his finger at me, 'no matter how fierce the currents, everything will reach the Bay of Panormitis! Such is the power of the God!' He crossed himself again and looked at us quizzically. 'You believe in the God?' he asked in a low voice, 'you are believers?' We nodded. '*Bravo!*' he said. 'Then pray to him that

through his Archangel Michaelis he will answer my prayers.'
Involuntarily Maria fingered the gold cross which hung around
her neck. 'What prayers?' she asked, 'for what do you pray?'
Manolis's eyes misted. 'For my daughter,' he said. 'She too is
a Maria you understand;' and he took her hand and held it.

His daughter, he told us, suffered from deep depression.
For the past two months no words had passed her lips. Nor
had she smiled but daily sat in a darkened room and cried
and cried. *Ne*, doctors had seen her, many many times – and
at some expense; but none could help her. The problem they
had told him was not in her body but in her mind. But that he
knew; and why. She had lost her faith in God and all because
her *ghataki* – her little cat – had died choking on a fish bone.
She was, we must understand, thirteen and had just reached
puberty – that was perhaps contributing to her condition; but
to reiterate, he knew the real reason. She had rejected God.
And so he prayed and would pray for her redemption in the
monastery of the Archangel Michaelis.

There was a long silence and half a league passed under
our keel. Then, over the waves faintly but growing stronger
as the distance closed came the sound of bells and the cries of
geese. '*Ne*,' said Manolis, 'Panormitis.'

We kept our promise and prayed for Michaelis and his
daughter. In the chapel of the monastery and surrounded by
the icons of bygone saints we lit three candles, one for each
of us and one for Manolis's daughter, and sat contemplatively
in the wooden stalls of olive wood with our arms resting on
the well-worn chest-high supports polished with the patina
of ages, and in the candles' flickering light and that from a
low-powered central candelabra we looked upon a faded full
figure of the Archangel Michael illustrated on the exquisitely decorated iconostasis, the sanctuary screen. But it was
Manolis who occupied our attention. Kneeling before it,
his back toward us as he prayed, his shoulders heaved and
shook but no sound came from him. And when in silence
we left him to his private grief our own cheeks were wet,
for some of his sadness had brushed off on us. However,

and thanks in no small measure to Mains Razor, our gloom was soon lifted.

Instructed to return to the ship for luncheon and a one thirty sailing for Tilos, we re-embarked in twos and threes, and at the appointed hour anchor chains rattled in the deep, plates clattered in the galley and with screws turning and its gangway hoisted the *Ismeni* got under way. Next to us and in company with several others including the Stallion of the Sea, the Great Sport clicked away with her Pentax as the stretch of water opened out and then gave a shout.

'My God!' cried she, lowering her camera and gesticulating to the shore. 'We've gorn without Mains Razor! Look! He's with two women over there! Ha! Ha! Ha! Poor old josser!' 'Damn!' said the Stallion turning puce with rage. 'Damn! Damn! Damn! I knew we'd have trouble with him! Probably been looking for a plug for his bloody razor!' And rushing up to the bridge and colliding with Takis who was on his way down to find out the cause of the hubbub, he ordered the engines to be stopped. Meanwhile, away on the quay Mains Razor, accompanied by the Lady with the Lump and an overweight superannuated ex-ballet dancer, continued to engage our attention.

Seen through a binocular unselfishly loaned to me by Cynthia, the Fortnum and Mason's sweetmeat seller, he appeared to be quite unmoved by the turn of events and was showing no emotion, although seemingly a trifle unsteady on his feet. Not so his companions who, flanking him, were giving a creditable if unsynchronised rendition of a Maori war dance, the like of which I had not seen since that performed by the All Blacks at Twickenham prior to their encounter with an English fifteen. It was an interesting spectacle and one which fortunately attracted the attention of a man and child in a passing rowing boat. Together we watched it draw alongside the harbour wall, observed the delinquent trio clamber uncertainly into the rocking craft and gave a cheer as the boatmen bent to his oars. 'By 'eck,' said Walter-call-me-Wally as the human cargo was ferried toward us, 'that feller's earning his money – must be near on 'alf a ton of flesh in that boat. And by gow,' he added observantly, 'aintit got lumpy?' 'Quite so,' agreed the Stallion primly, and gave orders for the aluminium rope-railed steps to be slung down the side of the ship.

Walter was correct. The sea had become choppy and it was with considerable difficulty that the Lady with the Lump made the short transition between the pitching boat and the foot of the far from stable ladder, even when aided by the helping hand of the Stallion who gallantly had positioned himself three-quarters of the way down the steps. Equal old-world courtesy was extended to the ex-ballet dancer who, similarly maladroit, palpably demonstrated to her audience that her footwork was not as it was when once she had *jetéed* lightly around the banks of Swan Lake; but it was Mains Razor who made the major contribution to the pre-luncheon entertainment.

Thrice he rose uncertainly from his seat and thrice returned heavily and unceremoniously to it. A fourth effort proved equally fruitless but at his fifth attempt miraculously he defied the laws of gravity and for a few seconds swayed in an upright position to wild applause from his fellow passengers. 'Well done!' cried the Stallion, bravely advancing two steps further down the ladder and extending his arm, 'now grab hold of this.' 'My dear feller,' puffed Mains Razor, 'how very kind,' and pulled him into the sea.

As the Great Sport said when, in the words of the Harvest Hymn, all was safely gathered in, we should not have laughed, but we did.

The afternoon passed quietly and without further excitement apart from that occasioned by the herb-allergic lady who, at luncheon, found a stray piece of oregano in her personalised salad and consequently had to retire to her berth with misted spectacles and in a state of shock. Meanwhile the remainder of the company, replete with roughage and assorted cold meats, settled down to a period of meditation or indolence. Walter inflated his lilo and lay upon it like a beached white whale; the Stallion reappeared wearing dry clothing and a smile of qualified forgiveness, and Mains Razor, slumped in a canvas

111

. . . pulled him into the sea . . .

chair, addressed himself to a bumper book of crossword puzzles which he appeared to read rather than solve. Minutes later he fell asleep with his mouth wide open and a large bread crust adhering to the underside of his moustache, where it stayed *in situ* for forty-eight hours and prompted the Great Sport to open a book on the reasons for its tenacity. At four o'clock prompt, lemon tea and pastries were served to those still in need of restoratives, an English ritual which the Pigs Robinson patronised with enthusiasm, and two hours later Manolis hailed us from the bridge. '*Ella!*' he called, 'come!'; and pointed for'ard. 'Tilos,' he shouted.

In the middle distance and bathed in the rays of a low-lying sun which hung over gentle hills and cut a spangled sword across a garnet sea, we watched the plum-coloured silhouette of Tilos grow larger against a pale blue sky shot with pink. And as we neared the island which with tiny Nisyros further north serves as a giant's stepping stone to Kos, it seemed that its peaks reached out toward the sun and drew it even closer to them. It was very beautiful.

'*Ne*,' said Manolis morosely and easing the wheel a fraction to starboard as we voiced our opinion, 'but it looks more beautiful than it is. Stones,' he continued gloomily, 'stones and rocks – that is all it is. To grow a vegetable there is a miracle. *Ne*, I tell you if you would wish to be buried there you would have to bring your own soil. *Ne*, it is true. It is a useless place of no importance. One ruined town, one main road, two villages with perhaps three or four hundred people, that is Tilos – an island of ghosts.'

'*Oche*,' said Sotiris benignly, tentatively turning the wheel to port, 'it is not so bad. After all,' he added, hurriedly removing his hand as Manolis testily readjusted our course, 'did they not find the bones of small elephants there ten years ago?' Manolis's face set in a mask of disbelief. 'Elephants?' he said, '*small* elephants?' '*Ne*,' repeated Sotiris earnestly, 'very old small elephants.' 'And of what use', asked Manolis sourly, 'are the bones of very old small elephants? Tell me that? Sotiris looked blank. '*Ksero*,' he said, 'I don't know.' 'Then shut up', snapped Manolis and lapsed into silence. Clearly wounded, Sotiris shrugged his shoulders and stared hard at the deck. Then, his face brightening, he tapped Maria on the shoulder. 'The people there', he volunteered, 'are very friendly, very friendly indeed.'

Sotiris was correct. The natives were extremely friendly; and hospitable. Within minutes of entering the nearest *cafeneon* only a few steps from the quayside of Livadi, the settlement where we disembarked, we were plied with bottles and morsels of tinned and fresh fish, the *mynothis* – literally samples to 'satisfy the nose' – and the presence of two other Yannis, elderly, unshaven and grimy, and a pock-marked Maria presiding over the establishment added to the *bonhomie*. An hour later, and in the manner of a gunman entering a Wild West saloon, the Great Sport burst through the rickety door. 'Hi!' she trumpeted, arrowing her way toward us and our table companions where, thus acknowledged as a friend of ours, she was pronounced good, embraced and quickly sucked into the social hub.

'Can't understand a word of the lingo,' she shrilled as the glub-glub-glub from a retsina bottle announced the freshening of her glass, 'but they're super people, don't you think?' And emptying her tumbler in the twinkling of an eye she exploded into a rendering of 'Land of Hope and Glory' in a remarkably true contralto voice, and did a little dance. '*Bravo!*' cried one and all, and proffered her more fish.

She was still in high spirits when we left. 'Aah!' chorused our hosts as we bade our farewells. 'The old one has the *kephi*, the joy, the essence of life – may the Blessed Saint Christopher and all the saints go with her on her travels!' '*Episis*,' we cried on her behalf, 'and with you.' 'I think', murmured Maria perceptively, as we crossed the earth road to the *Ismeni*, 'that it would be a good idea if I lent her an arm!' I nodded. 'Yes,' I agreed, 'I think it would,' and watched them precede me.

In retrospect it was unfortunate that we became separated. Trailing in their wake and easing my way through the assorted gathering of locals assembled around the *Ismeni*, summarily

I was accosted by a middle-aged man of lowly stature and, as it transpired, incapable of speech. Smiling at me politely with closed lips but quickly broadening the gesture into a leer to display a half-set of stained teeth, silently he mouthed a greeting. Then, coquettishly pressing his hands and fingers together and inclining his head, he placed them against his cheek, fluttered his eyelids, leered again and jerked his thumb toward the east. His message was unmistakable. I fled up the gangway, missing my footing as I went.

It was a bizarre encounter and one which occupied my dreams that night and invaded my thoughts during the short eight-mile passage to Nisyros the following morning. There, excluding ourselves and the Great Sport who employed her time by diving into the waters of its harbour, Mandraki, and emerging with stentorian cries of 'come on in – it's simply spiffing in here, don't you know', the rest of our companions made an excursion to the highest point of the island, Mount Diabates. Three hours later they returned from it volcanic rim smelling strongly of sulphur and, in the case of Mains Razor who, inadequately clad in tennis shoes, had ventured too close to its active lava crust, burning rubber.

'By 'eck,' said Walter joining the semi-circle of four who out of prudent curiousity had gathered to watch Mains Razor sit down and remove the sticky and charred remains of his Korean-made footwear, 'it's gone right through to 'is sock! And doesn't he pong?'

Mains Razor eyed him balefully and carefully peeled off his anklet to reveal two large angry blisters. 'And', continued Walter bending down to peer more closely at the purple blebs, 'I'd pop those before supper if I was you. Oh aye,' he reiterated slowly as he straightened up, 'pop 'em, that's what I'd do. I had a cousin', he enlarged ponderously, 'who didn't pop a blister. And do you know what happened?' 'No,' breathed his audience antiphonally, 'what?' 'She swelled up in t'groin, that's what,' said Walter, 'just like a balloon.'

Mains Razor blinked at him disbelievingly. 'My dear

115

fellow,' he quavered, 'you don't say.' And displaying considerable anxiety he hobbled away to his cabin.

'Have you done it?' inquired Walter indelicately over dinner. 'Have you popped 'em?' Mains Razor slowly put down his knife and fork. 'I have,' he confirmed but showing little appetite for the subject as a topic to accompany his risotto, 'and thank you for your advice.' 'That's good,' said Walter, 'then you'll not swell up.' 'No,' said Mains Razor with commendable restraint, 'I shall not, as you put it, swell up.' But he was still walking like a distressed penguin when we left for Kephalos after breakfast.

Kephalos on the west side of Kos was well known to us from previous visits to the island as was Kardamena in the south, and the memories of that once sleepy fishing village flooded back as we sailed slowly past it two miles out and along the coastline which we knew so intimately. Consequently it came as a surprise to us when predictably Kephalos came into view on our starboard beam but then dropped behind. 'I think', said Maria after a moment's reflection, 'that we're about to run out of coast.' Ten minutes later we were joined hurridly by Manolis with Takis hard on his heels.

Agitatedly and in silence they scanned what remained of Kos. Then: 'tell me,' said Manolis, 'you know the island?' We nodded. 'And Kephalos?' We nodded again. 'Then where is it?' he asked. 'Sotiris cannot find it on the chart.' Silently we pointed aft. 'Over there,' we said. 'We passed it some time ago.'

The scene that followed into which the Stallion, alerted by the raised voices, was drawn, was not a happy one. Takis questioned Manolis's legitimacy and his IQ for having allowed Sotiris to plot our course unsupervised, Manolis in turn cast doubts upon Takis's parentage and threatened to resign, and Kos slipped further and further away as the exchanges continued on ever rising cadences. 'Gentlemen! Gentlemen!' cried the Stallion, fearful that the altercation should spread disquiet among his charges, 'forget it! It doesn't matter! Just carry on to Kalymnos as if nothing had happened! That is', he muttered

116

. . . walking like a distressed penguin . . .

to us in an aside, 'if they know where *that* is.' He mopped his brow, watched the disgruntled and still seething ones return to the bridge and turned to Maria. 'And now', said he, 'you know why it is that we never sail at night . . .'

Gradually the sounds of acrimony from the bridge died down as in the manner of all Greek arguments the verbal storm abated as quickly as it had broken. On deck the prostrate bare-backed bodies of the Pigs Robinson and Walter continued to turn pink under thin cloud and a hazy sun, and by one o'clock we docked safely in the port of Kalymnos' largest town, Pothnia.

'*Endaxi?*' shouted the now pardoned Sotiris, beaming at us from the wheelhouse as we looked across to the tiers of neo-classical brightly painted houses set amphitheatrically against a backdrop of hills, and at the line of shops and *tavernas* along its front, '*Ine kala, ne* – it is good, eh?' '*Ne,*' we yelled back above the sounds of canned bouzoukoi music and the roar of traffic, 'but noisy.' '*Symphono,*' bellowed Sotiris as a stream of motor cycles roared along the quayside, 'I agree. It is the sponge-divers you understand – they have come back with their sponges and now they get drunk!' And he grinned and rubbed his finger and thumb together. '*Ine poli lepta etho,*' he said, 'there is plenty of money here – because of the sponges.'

It was an opinion later endorsed by Manolis and Takis as in the early evening we sat together in a *taverna* on the restless, bustling waterfront and watched a seemingly endless cavalcade of Suzukis and Hondas rev past us. '*Ne,*' said Manolis, 'there is much wealth here from sponge fish-ing. Each April you understand, these people leave for the Mediterranean and every October, like now, they come back to feastings and so on. At least,' he qualified, 'some do, but not all. *Oche!* There are those who never come back. *Ne*, it is a dangerous business this diving.' And he stared gloomily into his glass and then at Maria.

'Do you know', he asked her, 'what they call the night before they sail to Africa? Have you heard the name?' She shook her head. '*Ipnos tis Agapis,*' he said, 'the Sleep of Love. But I tell you Maria, for some', and here he crossed himself, 'it is the last time they lie in a woman's arms.' '*Ne*,' echoed Takis, 'it is true. Look around the town before we leave and you will see how many young women there are dressed in black. Po! Po! Po! But always', he continued, 'it has been like this on Kalymnos, for a century perhaps.'

'And a hundred years ago', enlarged Manolis, 'they did not have the diving helmets, you understand. *Oche!* No, they dived naked with a great stone around their necks – a *kambanellopetra* it was called.' '*Ne*,' rejoined Takis, 'and on Simi there is a special song about this stone. "To the sea I owe my body," they sing, "and to the air my soul, but my *life* hangs on the *kambanellopetra*." *Ne*, those are the words the divers sing and – '

'*And*,' interrupted Sotiris excitedly and displaying surprising erudition, 'I will tell you what the women reply!' And placing his hands upon his hips and raising his voice to a shrill falsetto above the traffic noise he sang, 'I wish I was a *kambanellopetra* hanging around your neck and filling your heart and thoughts.'

A short silence followed Sotiris's dying notes. Then: '*Mana mou*,' said Takis, clearly put out that his thunder had been stolen by a junior employee, 'you sounded like a *poushtie!*' 'Maybe,' said Sotiris, leering at a passing well-endowed young girl dressed in red, 'but I wouldn't mind changing *her* into a *kambanellopetra*.' And he nudged me in the ribs and brayed loudly into the evening air. 'I tell you, Yanni *mou*, daily she could hang around my neck – *and* through the night as well! Huh! Huh! Huh!' He had a simple sense of humour but his carnality injected a welcome flippancy into the conversation. Even Manolis mustered a smile . . .

By seven o'clock all had returned to the *Ismeni* and all carried sponges of assorted sizes, shades and forms. The Great Sport nursed a monstrous honey-coloured creation, Mains Razor a no less well-developed fan-shaped example, and Walter, fingering a lesser exhibit with a hole in it, said he knew it would last him a lifetime and give him untold pleasure in his bath. Only the lady allergic to herbs returned empty-handed. The odour of sponges, she advised us prissily, caused her nose to prickle and her eyes to smart. Consequently, surrounded as she was by the smells from these fruits from the deep, it came as no surprise when she absented herself from the dinner table, despite being offered the use of a nasal inhalant by the unsmiling Patience, who declared that she knew exactly how she felt as she had an aunt who was similarly affected by loofahs.

Leaning over the rail after dinner, during which Patience, inspired by the memory of her aunt, concentrated the conversation wholly upon the preservation and deodorising of sponges, we looked out at the throbbing town ablaze with lights and neon signs and listened to its sounds. Now more noisy and frenzied than in the early evening, added to the cacophony of motor horns and engines came the tannoyed voices of champions of the Greek Communist Party as they rallied on the front. '*Exo! Exo!* Karamanlis!' they blared through the speakers and railed against the incumbent President to a background of music by Theodorakis, the poet darling of their party who had suffered so cruelly under the Colonels. 'Out! Out! Karamanlis!' '*Ne!*' roared the excited and sizeable crowd gathered around a rostrum crudely painted with the hammer and sickle and the letters KKE in red. 'Out! Out! Out!' And an orchestrated chant of *Ku! Ku! A! Ku! Ku! A!* rose and fell like a turbulent wave.

'Po! Po! Po!' said Manolis as he stopped by on his way to his cabin and looked at the assemblage of waving clenched fists. 'They are fools you understand, these *Ku Ku As* – imbeciles and agnostics! But they are right about Karamanlis – the New Democratia have done nothing for us. *Tipota! Ne*, for myself I shall vote for Papandreou and Pasok at the General Election. *Ne*, I tell you, Yanni, by the end of this month we shall have the first Socialist Government in Greece! But this lot?' He dismissed them with a smack of his hands. '*Scoopedia!*'he said. 'Rubbish!' And he gave five fingers toward them. 'But,' I said as another roar of approbation reached us, 'they have their followers?' '*Ne,*' agreed Manolis grudgingly, 'in all the islands you find a few communists. Even in Patmos. And *that* is a holy place. *Ne,*' he affirmed, flicking his butt end over the side, 'Patmos is a godly island. But that', said he, 'you shall see when we go there. *kali nichta ke o Theos mazi su* – and the God be with you.' Five paces from us he stopped and turned. 'Do not forget my Maria in your prayers,' he said, and went below.

The sun shone kindly upon us as we left the clamour of Kalymnos behind us next morning and crossed the narrow strait to Telendos, and thence to sleepy Lipsos north-west of Leros, but early on Monday when we weighed anchor and sailed for Patmos the weather broke and the wind rose. For an hour and a half the *Ismeni* pitched, tossed and corkscrewed with groaning timbers through seas far removed from those pictured in glossy brochures, and on the bridge Messrs Manolis, Sotiris and Takis crossed themselves repeatedly. In the saloon the Lady with the Lump turned green, Patience clasped her stomach and from the galley came the crash of breaking crockery and glass followed by Antipodean oaths as Sophie and Bettina precariously went about their business. Even the Great Sport was subdued and it was with undisguised relief that we made our anchorage.

That Pathos was an island steeped in the history of the Christian faith was immediately apparent. A large notice erected in front of one of the restored, square, whitewashed Seventeenth-century houses bore testimony to that. 'Welcome to Patmos,' it read, 'but please respect our traditions,' and the deep-toned bells tolling from the Byzantine fortress monastery of Saint John the Theologian, which has dominated the port from the heights of the old town of Chora since the twelfth century, emphasized the accent on the spiritual. However, within minutes of elbowing our way through the streets of Skala with its plethora of hotels, *tavernas* and American and German tourists who had swarmed ashore from a visiting cruise ship, it became evident that the blessed isle had learned to serve both God and Mammon.

Boldy exhibited in the window of a side-street bookshop

clearly owned by an eclectic, a volume on the life of Saint John the Evangelist shared pride of place with a lesser work entitled *Dinosaur Planet*, while a richly illustrated book on icons was displayed next to a Swedish publication graphically exampling the virtues of nudity. Equally determined to show his catholicity to prospective clients was the proprietor of a restaurant, a Mr Stelios. Listed among the many cocktails advertised on a board outside his establishment was Ouzo Revelation under which a former patron had written irreverently and in English – 'as drunk and concocted by Saint John himself'. Nor after climbing the steep windswept road to the upper town did we find a remarkable sense of piety in the little chapel next to the cave in which the Evangelist, so legend has it, heard the thunderous voice of God and saw his vision of the Apocalypse. Maybe that cave, its walls now blackened with the smoke from oil lamps hanging from its ceiling, was the place from where John's message to the seven churches in Asia originated, but the cold, unwelcoming priest reading a paperback western at its entrance did little to help us conjure up the ghosts of AD 95. But at least our visit spurred me to reread the words of the Divine's Revelation that night.

'I am Alpha and Omega, the first and the last,' he dictated to his pupil Prochoros, the voice of God still fresh in his ears: 'and, what thou seest, write in a book.'

I put a marker in the Bible, shut it and put my hands behind my head. 'Do you believe', I asked Maria in the top bunk, 'that it really was God talking to him?' 'I don't know,' she said, stifling a yawn. 'But I think it more likely that he was hallucinating. After all,' she said with professional acumen, 'he'd had little to eat for a hell of a time. But I don't think it really matters, do you? Surely the importance is that the book was written.' She yawned again and stretched her hand over the side of her bunk. 'Goodnight love,' she said, 'God bless' . . .

The high winds which had gusted and blown us into Patmos and raised the white dust in its streets faced the *Ismeni* as she rolled towards Samos, and only Maria, the Great Sport and myself braved the elements to watch its mountains come up like ghosts through the lowering clouds with Icaria to the west and Turkey to the east. It was an unpleasant journey punctuated by moans and invocations from the supine saloon or bunk-bound passengers and we docked with difficulty and varying degrees of pallor. Few, including the Pigs Robinson, took advantage of luncheon and it was not until the later afternoon that most of the company ventured into Pythagoreion.

Like Skala in Patmos, Pythagoreion, named in honour of one of Samos's most famous sons, Pythagoras, was a busy tourist-orientated town with tourist-orientated prices, but the island has always been a venue for excursionists. Cleopatra for example, before she became obsessed with asps, spent many a happy hour in its verdant groves and valleys in company with Anthony, and the late Lord Byron, well known for his libidinous nature as well as an aptitude for writing verse, strongly approved of the local wine. 'Dash down', he cried, 'yon cup of Samian wine', and by all accounts did so, not infrequently. So did Mains Razor. Not too proud to take the advice of an old Harrovian he followed the noble lord's exhortation to the letter. Not once but many times did he fill the bowl and raise a beaker of the sweet Moschata to his lips, and he looked long and loving upon dry lesser reds as well. All, he advised us smilingly as he was assisted aboard by his female entourage and guided to his cabin, were very, very good.

Only Manolis was not amused, but nothing moved him to laughter that night. Morosely, and in company with Sotiris and Takis, he watched a half-moon lying on its back beyond the scudding clouds slip westward, and pontificated darkly about Turkey which we were due to visit on the morrow, and on the port of Kusadasi in particular. In 1974, he told us, he had been imprisoned there. 'You remember that year?' he asked us gloomily. 'When Turkey invaded Cyprus? Well, that was why I was arrested - because I was a Greek. *Ne*, for four days they kept me there. If I went ashore tomorrow I would show you the gaol, but I will not leave the boat while we are there. *Oche!* Not once! I am not afraid of the bastards, you understand, but I do not like their smell.' *'Ne,'* agreed Takis, 'it is well known that the Turks smell.' *'Oche,'* said Sotiris, 'they do not smell – they stink. But have you heard the news? Sadat has been assassinated. *Ne,* it was on the radio . . .'

Manolis was as good as his word. For the two nights we were in Kusadasi he never moved from the *Ismeni* but cross-examined us at length when we returned from our first evening meal in the town. 'Ah,' he said mournfully when we spoke of its spicy excellence and variety, 'believe me it will keep you on the lavatory for hours. *Ne,* it could even poison you.' And he shook his head. 'I knew a man', he continued, 'who died from eating Turkish chillies. And what of the people? Are they not as I told you, like beasts?'

As Maria remarked as we made ready for bed, it would have been heartless to have told him we found them delightful.

The Turks *were* charming. Young, middle-aged and sometimes quite elderly gentlemen with smiling dark eyes, heavy moustaches and close-cropped black hair flashed their teeth and beckoned us into doorways. 'Come,' they cooed with enticing old-world courtesy, and offering us innumerable cups of tea in tulip-shaped glasses together with sweet dry pastries encouraged us to buy second-hand carpets or meerschaum pipes, and in one case having established that Maria was childless guaranteed her immediate motherhood before sundown. However, despite this isolated lack of finesse, we enjoyed every minute of our encounters, but after only one excursion with Sotiris and Takis, through streets festooned with carcasses of sheep and goats which with freshly cut throats were being flayed in preparation for the Muslim feast of Kurban Bayrami,it was evident that Greeks were *personae non gratae* in Kusadasi. Dark looks and even worse gestures were given to our companions and they did not venture abroad again.

Few of our compatriots explored the town in depth. *En masse* and clutching packed lunches they set off first for Ephesus on the Thursday and then, on the following day, Didyma, from where they returned in the mid-afternoon tired, hot and dusty but with their cultural appetites satisfied. Of their activities on and about that sacred site we learned from the Great Sport that Mains Razor, finding the descent from the Temple of Apollo too steep, had hopped down the steps two at a time and on a rising staccato had broken wind at every jump, and that Patience, firmly believing in the aphrodisiacal properties of the Pool of the Blessed Virgin Mary, had immersed her feet in it despite the opinion of Walter that it would take more than those waters to cure *her* feet. Consequently, she told us, they were not speaking to each other.

An hour later, and with the Greeks behaving like schoolboys released from detention, we began our return crossing of the eighteen miles of water which separated Turkey from Samos. Sotiris and Takis sang all the way; Manolis, free from the shadow of the Turkish yoke, shed a hundred years, and with a light heart docked us neatly at Pythagoreion and jumped ashore together with his equally elated colleagues. 'I am', he advised all and sundry, 'going to get drunk.' *'Endaxi!'* affirmed Takis clapping him on the back. 'Truly we are home again! But do not forget, my friend,' he added, 'that we leave for Leros tomorrow – and the forecast is bad.'

The meteorologists were right. The weather was bad and worsened considerably over the next three days as we sailed southward, retracing our outward path. Leros, that quiet hilly neighbour of Kalymnos and the scene of carnage in 1941 when so many British lost their lives defending it, was reached and left with difficulty, and so too was Kos and Simi where we arrived at sundown on the Monday to accompanying rolls of thunder.

It seemed an age since the two of us in company with Messrs Hall, Waldo and Marvin of blessed memory had landed there to be taken under the wing of the neurotic Nikos Pipsos at the beginning of our brief sojourn on the island, but of our erstwhile friend we caught not a glimpse as we walked with Manolis to have a meal. What we did see was a rent-a-crowd crocodile of small boys snaking their ways through the streets before halting outside the house of the local *Neo Democratia* candidate. *'Boo! Boo! Boo!'* they chanted enthusiastically and well rehearsed, and then, their mission completed, dispersed to file past the back door of the Pasok headquarters to receive substantial *pourboires* for their services. 'You see,' said Manolis raising his voice above a thunder clap, 'as I told you in Samos, Pasok will win.'

'My God,' said Mains Razor when we went aboard with sheet lightening flashing behind the dark banks of clouds, 'what a bloody noise these wogs make, don't you think? What's all the fuss about?' I enlightened him. 'These wogs', I said, 'are about to elect a new government. Manolis thinks it may be a socialist one.' Mains Razor blinked at me. 'My dear feller,' he said, 'you don't say. Whatever will Thatcher think . . .?'

No one slept well that night and the storm which rumbled on into the small hours of the following morning trailed us fitfully as we ploughed through choppy seas and rain squalls for Rhodes and our journey's end. There, under a cloudy sky on a hot, humid afternoon we said farewell to our companions of the last twelve days before disembarking to spend the night with Yiorgo Zagorianos and Anna-Marie prior to returning to England. The Great Sport embraced us and offered us ever-lasting friendship, which she gave us until she died some five years later, Manolis thanked us for our prayers and dabbed his eyes with a dirty handkerchief, Patience ignored us and Mains Razor, clearly suffering from lack of sleep, raised his hat, extended his hand and asked us who we were. 'Goodbye!' cried the girls and the rest of the crew as we piled our luggage into a taxi. 'Let's hope we meet again!' And they waved us out of sight.

'In a funny way', said Maria as we were driven to Yiorgo's, 'I shall miss them.' 'Yes,' I said, 'so will I – in a funny way; especially Manolis. I wonder how his daughter is . . .'

8

The Birthplace of Zeus

It was seven months later that we were given news of Manolis's daughter. Quite by chance we happened upon him sitting alone in a café on the Rhodes waterfront drinking thick black coffee and letting the tourist world wash over him. '*Panayia mou!*' he cried when he saw and embraced us. 'All Holy Virgin! What are you doing here and how long are you staying?' 'Only today,' we told him; 'with Zagorianos. Tomorrow we go to Crete. But what of you, and how is your Maria?' 'Ah,' he said, brightening visibly as he ordered coffee, '*ine kala* – she is good,' and enlarged upon his daughter's change of fortune.

Once again, thanks be to the God he told us, she welcomed the priest, attended church and consequently her melancholia left her. As for himself, life was better. Pasok and Papandreou were in power as he had predicted they would be; he, having told Takis what to do with the *Ismeni*, was in happier employment and despite a dreadful stomach problem was facing the future stoically. He paused to flush down an anti-dyspeptic tablet. 'And so you', he asked rhetorically and grimacing as the pellet momentarily lodged on its downward journey, 'are you going to Crete?' We nodded. '*Bravo!*' he applauded. 'You will like the Cretans even if you cannot follow their Greek. They have a strange accent you understand. But they are a good people. *Ne*, they voted Pasok. And you my friend', he continued, addressing me directly, 'will remember their bravery in 1941, *ne*?' 'Yes,' I said, 'I remember it well.' And my mind went back to the dark dawn day of the 20th of May, that year when the rose-coloured Cretan skies darkened under the wings of German planes and the airborne invasion of the island began.

Manolis was right. We did embrace Crete. It is a dramatic island with a dramaturgic past. There, Zeus, son of Chronos and Rhea, was born in a cave in the thick forests under Mount Aegeum before being carried by his grandmother to the peak of Psiloritis in the central area of Rethymnon; there, fair-haired Theseus, born of a double union between his mother Aethra and Aegeus the mortal king of Athens and the god Poseidon, slew the maiden-devouring Minotaur in the labyrinth constructed by Daedalos; and there, as mythology melted into fact, the Cretans staged ten revolutions against the Turks during the ensuing centuries of their occupation. As wise old Homer wrote in his *Odyssey*, the Cretans, or as he called them, the Pelasgians, were a 'singular' people.

His adjective was apt. The Cretans were, and are, an individual breed of men. To be sure they are Greek, but primarily they are Cretan and display a fierce panache and pride. Full chested, sometimes pot-bellied and moustachoed, they face one aggressively with their arms hanging loosely by their sides as if waiting to draw imaginary pistols. 'Ya!' they rumble in deep voices roughed by *tsikouthia*, their steel-blue eyes glinting as they clasp one's hand in an iron embrace suggesting a test of manhood rather than a greeting, 'Yahara! Joy!' It took only a few days in the coastal village of Makriyalos in the south-east of Crete for us to recognise these traits. But it was not until the spring of 1985 when we paid the first of many visits to the south-west of the island, which on a map looks like a huge-headed prehistoric fish paddling through the Libyan Sea toward the Lebanon, that we found the true ethos of Crete.

The south-west of Crete is as untamed as the Cretans themselves. It is a region of deep ravines, gorges and wild mountainous scenery dominated by the high peaks of the Lefka Ori, the White Mountains, on whose cavernous slopes, the *andartes*, the guerrilla fighters fought and died so bravely during the German occupation; and many did die. There is not a village nestling in the foothills of that range that does not mourn the deaths of relatives – men, women and children – who were killed either by firing squad or while fighting as

. . . a fierce panache and pride . . .

partisans. Tiny settlements like Azogires and Kakodiki or, to use the Cretan dialect, Kakodichi, all paid a heavy price for their resolution, and in them, turbanned old men in dark baggy trousers tucked into high black boots and wearing *zopanis* the traditional embroidered jackets, remember the horrors and heroics in word and song. They do not, and will not, forget. Nor have memories been erased in Kandanos.

It was less than a fortnight after our arrival in Crete on the day when the Cretans commemorated their island's battle that we were taken to Kandanos. Half an hour's drive from Kakodiki, it is a resurrected little town lying in the shadow of a hill, the top of which is graced by a church, and a township which like the fabled Phoenix has risen from its ashes, for in 1941 Kandanos went up in a thick pall of smoke.

Accounts of its destruction differ. Some say that with clinical efficiency the Germans transported all the oil from the houses and refineries to the top of the hill, emptied the contents of the barrels so that the oil ran down in streams into the narrow streets below, and then set the flood ablaze. Others maintain that the town was dynamited systematically. Either way the carnage was great. But perhaps the story is told succinctly in an open space in Kandanos in the centre of the town. There, in the memorial ground to their dead and set in a long, rough-plastered turquoise wall are two plaques; both are inscribed in German and Greek. The first reads:

Here lies Kandanos. It was destroyed as a reprisal for the murder of twenty-five German soldiers.

The second, also written in Gothic script, translates:

For the bestial murder of German paratroopers, mountain troops and pioneers by men, women and children together with the priest, because they mounted resistance against the Great German Reich, Kandanos was, on the 3rd of June 1941, razed to the ground in order that it never again would be rebuilt.

Kandanos was rebuilt. Around it on the biscuit-coloured hillsides new vines and olive trees grow and there is peace and some prosperity, and a new generation walks its streets without fear. But the old, the survivors of that and other dreadful days, will always remember.

We will not easily forget that day we went to Kandanos. We drove there with friends from nearby Azogires, the village of 'everlasting life', and Paleochora on the coast where we had made our base, with: Little Yanni the van driver who delivered the beers; Papa Stylianos the fighter-priest; hawk-featured Eftichi who had led the partisans into the hills; his son Andonis whose uncle had been executed against a wall for hiding a New Zealander, and Erasmeia from our pension whose father had been shot out of hand in the fields around Kandanos. But hundreds made the pilgrimage. They went in klaxon-blaring buses, in crammed cars, in pick-ups filled with rush-seated wooden chairs in danger of collapse, on mopeds and motorbikes flying the Greek flag, and then by foot into the hot, dusty town itself.

There were hordes of us. Fierce-looking, bent-backed, extravagently moustachoed old men in traditional dress with scabbarded knives stuck in sashes or down the sides of their knee-high boots and leaning on crooked knobbly sticks of olive wood, aged black-draped women on walking-frames, children dressed in blue and white who had never known their grandfathers, and elderly bemedalled Antipodeans and Britons who, thanks to the Cretans, had lived to fight another day and had returned to pay homage to the dead and the living. *En masse* in a chattering noisy crowd we converged upon the town centre and then six deep, lined the four sides of the square festooned with plastic flags, which crackled in the wind like a volley of rifle fire, to listen to the service of remembrance relayed from the new church overlooking the arena, and the chanting of priests.

Next to me a man in his early thirties, his arm around a four-year-old girl straddled about his waist, drew his free hand across his eyes. I asked him from where he came. '*Apo etho,*' he said, 'from here, from Kandanos. My father was shot here with thirty others.' And his voice faltered as the first wreaths were laid and the ensign of New Zealand and the flags of Australia, Greece and Britain were dipped in salute before the tablets on the concrete wall.

There was a moment's silence. In front of us, overcome by the midday heat, a serviceman of the Greek Airforce fell as if pole-axed and still at attention. No one took heed of him and he lay there with his hat half on and his waxen face turned obliquely to the sun. The national anthems were sung, the prostrate one was carried away and then, as the tension broke, Cretans and Aussies, Kiwis and British rushed toward each other, embraced, and openly wept.

By British standards it was all over-emotional. As my father told me repeatedly, 'soldiers' sons don't cry', especially the sons of English soldiers. But we in Britain were fortunate. To be sure, we suffered the 'blitz' when the war arrived on our doorstep and rubbed our noses in it, but we were spared the horrors of seeing friends and relatives shot before us, which is why to the Cretans, anniversaries like that of Kandanos are not merely commemorations of events in the pages of a history book. The spilt blood is not yet dry . . .

The rememberance of that day did not end in Kandanos. That evening in Paleochora the main street was closed to traffic, tables were set out end to end in the roadway and flags were flown from every building. From an improvised platform erected next to a *taverna* and under a crudely painted poster depicting crouching partisans firing with outmoded rifles at falling paratroopers spewed out by low-flying Junkers 52s, came the amplified, plaintive hollow sound of the *lyra*, that most Cretan of all stringed instruments. '*Bravo!*' applauded the throng in the packed street as the last long drawn out note died away on a crotchet, and then fell silent as the town mayor delivered a passionate peroration extolling his country's resistance. It was a fine speech worthy of Pericles and the crowd roared their approval. Then, on to the rostrum came a group of five black-shirted moustached young men. All were dressed in national costume, all wore the *kefalomandilo*, the traditional black-crocheted head-covering of the Cretans, and they shook the air with their singing.

'When will the sky become clear', they sang, 'so that I will be able to take my rifle again, my beautiful *patrona?* I will go down to the mountain, to the village of Omalo and there I will make mothers without sons, women without husbands . . .'

It was a wild, revolutionary mountain-song which has been sung by the Cretans since the time they rose against the Turks and the singing was like the rumble of falling rocks. Their voices were deep and so too was the emotion they stirred and we were moved as we sat outside the *taverna* with Papa Stylianos and Little Yanni; but not so four young Germans at an adjoining table.

'Excuse me,' said one, a blonde youth in his late teens, stretching out his arm behind Maria and tapping me peremptorily on my left shoulder, 'you speak English I think, yes? So! Then tell me,' said he, pointing to the poster, 'what is all this business about? It is, I think, anti-German, yes?' 'Well,' I said, searching hard for a diplomatic answer, 'perhaps it would be more accurate to say that it is anti-Nazi.' And hiding my surprise at his ignorance of his country's recent history, gently I put him in the picture.

Cold blue eyes stared at me unblinkingly. 'Lies,' he said, 'all stupid lies. And I must tell you my friend that for my opinion this demonstration *is* anti-German.' Aggressively he jabbed the air with his forefinger as the singers reached a crescendo. 'And also,' he added, 'this is quite the most horrible noise. As for those ridiculous head-coverings . . .' He shrugged his shoulders, sneered, turned his back on me, related my explanation to his companions who sniggered behind their hands, and from then on mocked the quintet and the *lyra* player by putting their fingers in their ears until with an ill grace they flung some money on the table and swaggered off.

'All Holy Virgin!' said Papa Stylianos stroking his beard and following their exit through his glasses. 'They may be another generation but they do not change.' '*Ne*,' I said, 'I agree, but why do you welcome them here?' Papa Stylianos looked at me sideways, chuckled wheezily and put his hand on my arm. '*Yati?*' he said. 'Why? Because Yanni *mou* it is good for our economia. Oh yes! In these days the Deutschmark is just as good as sterling.' And he chuckled again. '*Ne,*' grinned Manolis, the *taverna* owner, collecting the scattered notes, '*ine etsi* – is is like that. And they tip well. So I smile at them, thank them and say come again. But,' he said as he swept the table clean with the palm of his hand, 'that is not to say that I like the bastards.' '*Ne,*' said Little Yanni employing the most common of Cretan insults, 'they are *keratas* – cuckolds!'

Little Yanni was a wiry, excitable, tiny widower no more than five feet three inches in height with well-greased, dyed black hair, a pencil-line and similarly doctored moustache and an enthusiasm for pungent deodorants. He also had a great regard for the priesthood. '*Kali nichta pater mou,*' he cried, jumping to his feet when close to midnight Papa Stylianos announced that the warm night air and dust was bringing on his asthma and that he was going to retire, 'may God and His angels attend you – and do not forget to inhale deeply on your breath machine. *Kalos hypnos* – sleep well.' '*Efharisto,*' said Papa Stylianos, '*episis* – and you; but at my age only naughty memories can keep me awake.' And he winked, made the sign of the cross over all of us and departed leaving Yanni to pay the bill.

'*Mana mou!*' said Little Yanni as he refused a contribution from us and settled with Manolis. 'What a man! He is retired now you understand and is devoting himself to writing a book about dirty Cretan jokes, but during the war – Po! Po! Po!' He flung his arms into the air and raised his eyebrows to the heavens. 'I tell you', he said, 'only the God knows how many of those *kallikantzaroi*, those demons, he killed with his old Martini rifle. Maybe thirty, forty, fifty he shot, perhaps even a thousand, but that is his secret. But,' he said, pausing to drain a neglected glass and rising to his feet, 'I too have a secret! *Ella!* Come!'

Slowly we walked through the emptying street to his

house, up the three steps to the vine-covered veranda and halted at the threshold of the living-room. 'Sh!' said Little Yanni tapping his nose, 'Sh! Sh!' And tiptoeing across the room with exaggerated caution, he led us to a large wooden chest. 'Sh! Sh!' he repeated, and unlocked it with a huge iron key. The unoiled hinge groaned as he raised the lid and peered into its interior. Then, reaching down, he lifted out a large heavy package swathed in black polythene held together with elastic bands, unwrapped the layers and there, greased and in perfect working order with four full magazines, was a German Schmeisser sub-machine-gun. 'There,' he said, holding the weapon to his shoulder and traversing the ceiling with it. 'Bam – bam – bam – bam – bam! *Ne!* My father took that from a paratrooper! *Ne!* He killed him. But before that, you understand, the man had shot my mother . . .'

That night was a warm one and there was the smell of jasmine in the air, but suddenly, or so it seemed to us, a chill came into the room.

Little Yanni was the first person we met in Paleochora and we warmed to him as readily as we did to most of the locals in that small coastal town. As Maria said when we approached it through the avenue of eucalyptus and mulberry trees which leads to its long main street lined by shops, *tavernas* and *cafeneons* and crowned by a ruined Venetian castle, 'it smelt right.' Instinctively we knew that we had come to a community which would find a place in our hearts, and time was to prove our initial feeling correct. Paleochora gave us a plethora of memories upon which to draw during an English winter: of mornings when before the sun had climbed too high we walked away from the town, picked our way along stony paths meandering in the lee of rocky hillsides thick with rose-pink oleander inhaled the heady scents of oregano, sage and thyme and then clambered down the slopes to a shingled shore to plunge into warm clear water and watch the sea-birds fishing; of early evenings when the sky was shot with purple and gold we would amble into the town and sit outside one-eyed Marko's *cafeneon* and drink a *tsikouthia* or two.

It was in Marko's that we first met Little Yanni and Papa Stylianos, who like many elderly priests of the Greek Orthodox Church, gave the impression of a black-draped, shop-soiled, out-of-season Father Christmas. Asthmatic and in his early seventies, grey bearded and with a dusting of dandruff on the collar of his robe, he was looking appreciatively through tinted spectacles at a girlie calendar upon the wall and flicking the pages with the top of his walking stick. 'Po! Po! Po!' he exclaimed as full-bosomed May gave way to buxom June and thence to braless July. '*Ine orea, ne?*' '*Ne,*' we agreed, 'very beautiful.' 'But,' he advised us as he bypassed August and moved to autumn, 'you should see November! Ho! Ho! Ho!' he wheezed, his shoulders shaking. 'All right! Yes!'

All right and yes were three of the four words which comprised Papa Stylianos's English vocabulary. The fourth was Montgomery. He had a huge esteem for the General and when I told him that I had met the Great Man his admiration was unbridled. 'Ah, Montgomery,' he cried, presenting arms with his stick and then crossing himself, '*ehi pai sto fengari, ne* – he has gone to the moon, yes? But what a man! Ah, if only we had had him here in 1941.' '*Ne,*' agreed Marko setting down our glasses of *tsikouthia* and a chipped saucer of nuts, 'and if only the Cretan division had been here we might have beaten the cuckolds.' I looked blank. '*Ne,*' explained Papa Stylianos, 'the Fifth Division – all our young men! They were stranded, you understand, in Greece on their way back from fighting in Albania against the *Macaronades* – the Italians. Everything was missing when it was wanted. Everything except courage.' '*Ne,*' chimed in Little Yanni reaching out for his glass, 'our General Metaxas had a lot to answer for. *Itane o hondrochefalos* – he was a thick head! *Lipon, panda irene* – here's to peace!' '*Irene?*' said Papa Stylianos cynically as we clinked glasses. 'Peace? Ho! Ho! Ho! *Tha to pistepso otan to tho* – I'll believe it when I see it.'

We became indebted to Papa Stylianos. It was he who helped us to come to terms with the soft 'che' of the Cretan dialect which replaced the hard 'k' of the Dodecanese and

'But you should see November!'

other islands and introduced us to local words and idiom. In Crete, he told us, the word *cheimonas* meaning winter was used to describe filthy weather regardless of the time of year; that when the days were sweaty, cloudy and humid we should say that it was '*nefokeima*'; that *melindachia* was the local word for flying ant. From him we learned that it is unlucky to sleep under a fig tree because the shadow it casts is heavy and induces dreadful dreams; that a lemon sprinkled with salt and sucked at the end of an evening of prolonged drinking prevents a hangover and, if that failed, a glass of *tsikouthia* tossed down at dawn when facing east will remedy the malady. And it was in the realm of Cretan toasts and drinking customs that he provided the most esoteric guidance.

'*Lipon* Maria *mou*,' he asked one night as we sat in Marko's with Little Yanni, 'do you know why it is that we clink our glasses?' '*Oche*,' she said, and shook her head, 'tell me.' 'Because', said Papa Stylianos, 'the five senses of man must be satisfied,' and he raised his glass to the light. 'First,' he said, 'the touch and the sight; then,' he continued, offering the vermouth to his nose and lips, 'the smell and taste; and now,' he concluded, tapping his glass against hers, 'the sound. Tok! Tok!' '*Bravo!*' said Little Yanni following suit, 'and now tell them about *kalogeristika!*' 'Ah ha' said Papa Stylianos helping himself to a nut. '*Ne! Kalogeristika* – to drink like the monks!' And encircling the tiny thick glass with his fingers and bidding me to do likewise, noiselessly and with only our knuckles touching we toasted each other in silent salutation. 'Sh! Sh!' said Papa Stylianos. 'Now the abbot won't hear us!' '*Ne*,' echoed Little Yanni placing his fingers to his lips and peering furtively around him. 'Sh! Sh! Sh!'

It was childish, but great fun. So too was the custom to which he introduced us, of drinking like little frogs – *ta vatrachakia* – when he held our glasses by the upper rims away from us, gently bounced the bottoms and sides together three times and let the clicks ring out like the distant croaking of frogs. 'Cro-ak!' we would cry in unison. 'Cro-ak! Cro-ak!' and Marko would look upon us with his one good eye, smile indulgently, top up our glasses and say, '*Bravo pethia mou* – well done my children!' But Papa Stylianos did more than admit to us the secrets of ritual drinking. He made us aware of the efficacy of prayer and of his influence with the saints. Papa Stylianos helped me to recover my teeth.

It was in the late afternoon of the last day of May that fortune turned her back on me, a day when suddenly and dramatically the weather changed and the hitherto placid sea in which we were swimming was rolled into motion by a westerly wind. On the horizon a deep blue hazy line appeared and I called across the water to Maria and pointed to it. 'Look!' I shouted, 'I think there's a storm in the offing.' It was the last articulate remark I was to make for some time. As I opened my mouth for an intake of air prior to repeating my opinion, a large truculent wave struck the side of my face with great force, and my upper set, gleaming white under the Aegean sun, flew across the churned-up surface and with a dreadful plop sank without trace to the invisible sea-bed some fifteen feet below.

Maria was very good. Lesser women faced with the prospect of being harnessed to a gummy companion for the forseeable future would have abandoned me but she remained loyal and practical. At her insistence and to furnish my insurance company with written proof of my loss, we made our way to the police station to report the incident; but the promise of not being able to talk coherently in English let alone Greek, of nothing more solid than yoghurt passing my lips for the remainder of our stay, filled me with gloom en route and I would not be comforted.

Understandably the *gendarmerie* were a little non-plussed. 'Teeth?' they repeated disbelievingly. 'You have lost your *teeth?*' Never, they advised us, had they recorded such a loss. Rings, watches, cameras and even a wife – to be sure they were familiar with things such as these – but *teeth*, and they called their superior to share the novelty. But they were very sympathetic and kind. They waited until the door had closed behind us before going into hysterics, but their laughter followed me into the street. However, Messrs Marko, Little Yanni and Papa

Stylianos were less considerate. Collectively and uninhibitedly they rolled about before us and slapped their knees and thighs. '*Mana mou!*' cried Little Yanni. 'Now you cannot bite Maria's ear!' And convulsed by his own fantasy and dodging Maria's open hand he buried his face in his arms.

'Never mind,' wheezed Papa Stylianos when he had dried his eyes and used his inhaler. '*Mi chirotera* Yanni – it could be worse. You still have the teeth God gave you in your bottom jaw – you can scrape *paximathia* across them like a rasp and eat the crumbs!' '*Ne,*' endorsed Marko giving me a consolatory glass of *tsikouthia*, 'like fat Yiorgo's father does in Azogires – and he has only two teeth in the whole of his head. And', he added, 'there is always *yohourti* and honey to keep you strong. Fat Yiorgo's father has eaten nothing but breadcrumbs, *yoghourti* and honey for years and he is still strong enough to please his wife!' '*Ne,*' agreed little Yanni, 'and he is a hundred and *two*. And do not forget Yanni *mou*, you can still drink! So *pandaya*, my friend, *pandaya!*' I sucked heavily upon my denuded gums, breathed deeply, and said nothing.

Supper that night was a melancholy meal. Fond as I am of *tzatziki*, that delicious dish of yoghurt, cucumber and garlic, after three platefuls even that palled and I looked longingly and frustratedly towards Maria's skewered *souvlaki*. Nor was I afforded relief through sleep for I was plagued by horrid dreams and mocked and ridiculed in my restless subconscious. As I tossed and turned between my tangled sheets itinerants from nearby villages, Germans and other tourists all had me pointed out to them as a curiosity. 'There,' they were told, 'you see that man? That is Yanni the Englishman whose teeth were swallowed by a large fish! *Ne*, by a huge *singritha!* Observe how his trousers are held up by string because of his shrinkage, for he now eats only crumbs and pulverised olives, you understand. *Ne*, like fat Yiorgo's father in Azogires only this weak one can please no woman. *Oche!* Indeed they say that his Maria has gone off with Andreas the tomato-grower from Gavdos because of such things. *Ne!* And notice too how, with so little food in his belly to absorb the ouzo, hourly he is a little drunk and sometimes falls down. *Ne! Ne! Ne!* It is true! Ask Papa Stylianos – he saw him do such a thing in front of the *cafeneon* and now prays for him. Po! Po! Po!' And so the nightmare continued, and I longed for dawn.

For two days and nights I mourned the loss of my dentures and then, on the evening of the third day as we sat morosely in Marko's *cafeneon*, the improbable happened. Weaving his way unsteadily from the direction of the sea and waving a blue polythene bag around his head came one Michaelis, a fisherman, who earlier in the day had dedicated first his eyes to Maria and then, two beers later, more private parts of his body. Clearly he was still euphoric.

'By all the saints,' muttered Marko out of the corner of his mouth as Michaelis came into the home stretch, 'he's *methismenos!*' '*Ne,*' said Little Yanni consulting his Mickey Mouse watch, 'of course he is – it's half past six.' 'Of course,' confirmed Papa Stylianos, 'all the world knows that daily Michaelis is drunk by this hour. *Yasu* Michaelis!'

'Ah,' said Michaelis crossing himself uncertainly and kissing the extended priestly hand, '*yasu pater mou. St-st-sto kalo* – go to the good!' '*Efharisto poli,*' said Papa Stylianos a little acidly, 'thank you very much but I am not going anywhere. But what is your news my son?' 'Ah,' repeated Michaelis taking two steps backward and then three forward as if embarking upon the cha-cha-cha, 'I have great news! Great news for Yanni! *Ne koumbari mou,*' he said swaying before me and smiling happily, 'I have brought you a present from the god of the sea!' And plunging his hand deep into his bag with all the panache of a conjuror, he produced my upper set.

I gazed at it incredulously. 'This', I lisped to an equally wide-eyed Maria, 'I do not believe.' '*Ne,*' roared Michaelis holding the stained trophy aloft and displaying it to the street, 'your teeth, your teeth! I saw them below me as I swam this afternoon. I was looking for an octopus, you understand, and there they were – grinning at me from the sea bottom! Now put them in Yanni, affix them in your mouth!' '*Ne,*' shouted a group of well-wishers at the next table and others across the

141

. . . waving a blue polythene bag . . .

road as I looked lovingly at my dentures, 'put them in, put them in! Now you can chew again Yanni, but oh my God you have looked funny without them!' Uncaring of the taste of stale brine and to wild applause I did as I was bid. *'Bravo, bravo!'* cried one and all, and led by a beaming if unstable Michaelis toasted my teeth to the skies.

'*Ne,*' said Papa Stylianos when the clapping had died down, 'and *bravo* Michaelis! But do you know', he asked of me, 'who led *him* to your teeth?' *'Oche,'* I said, happy and confident once again. 'Tell me.' Papa Stylianos tapped the side of his nose. 'The blessed Saint Anthony,' he said. 'And do you know why? Because', said he answering his own question, 'I have prayed three times a day to him, for *he* finds everything. *Ne* Yanni, *ine sosta* – as I am sitting here that is true.' And he raised his glass and winked at me. 'So,' he said, *'bravo* Ayios Andonis and *bravo* Papa Stylianos!' He paused, then raised his glass again. '*Ne,*' he said, *'yati oche* – why not? And *bravo* Montgomery! Ho! Ho! Ho! All right, yes?' 'Yes,' I said, 'very all right.'

9

Fiestas, Fusillades and Fate

They were happy times, those spring and autumn days in Paleochora. We saw mild-mannered May give way to the growing heat of June and then to kinder September, and we stayed on during the *microteri*, the short days of October and November when nets were spread in olive groves to catch the ripening harvest and the first heavy raindrops dented the earth and freshened the air.

We walked through all weathers: under cloudless skies and those heavy with mischief and with no promise for the morrow; on days when Boreas, the north wind of antiquity, first son of Eos the dawn and Astraeus the starry sky, whipped the silver-grey olive trees into subjugation; and on others so still that the air shimmered and vibrated with the hum of insects and the stridulating chorus of hidden cicadas. We watched the May picking of the tomato crops as they turned from yellow to red under the huge polythene-sheeted greenhouses on the outskirts of the village, and the September gathering of the grapes. We were there when the *frangosiko*, the prickly pear, burst into yellow flower; when the first swallowtail butterflies began their short lives and danced and fluttered in couples on the breeze; and when the swallows built their mud nests under eaves and balconies and later swooped in to feed their piping young. *Chelindonakia* they were called and welcomed as early summer guests but many were still there when the first snow capped the highest mountains at the end of October.

Little Yanni had such a family living under the faded blue-painted ceiling of his veranda. 'Ah,' he sighed, one evening in May as the morning-coated parent birds rested and twittered on the telephone wires stretching above our heads, *'chelindonaki mou gongo* – my swift little swallow. My grandfather used to sing a song of that name but it was a very difficult one and defeated me. But Papa Stylianos can sing it. *Ne,* he has a beautiful voice you understand, even with his asthma, and knows three hundred Cretan songs. *Ne!* More than any man in the whole of Crete! But *pethia mou,* you should hear him sing!' And he closed his eyes and raised his brows to the swallows. 'Po! Po! Po!' he said. 'Po! Po! Po!'

I looked first at Maria, and then at Little Yanni. *'Ella,'* I said, beckoning him closer, 'do you think Papa Stylianos would sing for us tomorrow?' Little Yanni looked puzzled. *'Avrio?'* he repeated, *'yati avrio* – why tomorrow?' 'Because,' I said, 'tomorrow is Maria's birthday.' 'Ahhh!' cried he jumping to his feet and embracing her, *'Bravo! Bravo!* Of course he will! I will see that he does! *Ne,* we shall have a *glendi* – a party! *Ne,* at my village, at Kakodieki, with my friends there. And,' he added excitedly, raising his sights from the plains of hedonism to more spiritual heights, 'I will show you the churches of Kakodiki. *Ne,* the most ancient chapels in the area! You will like that, yes?' 'Yes,' we said, 'we will.' *'Endaxi,'* said Little Yanni, and standing on tiptoes kissed Maria again. 'Tell me,' he asked, 'how old will you be tomorrow . . .?'

Even the gods heralded Maria's natal celebrations. On the following morning at seven thirty precisely as I responded unwillingly to the pip-pip-pip of my digital alarm and crossed the tiny room in our pension to awaken her, somewhere below our planet's crust Rhea, the Cretan earth-goddess, stirred in her sleep. Then, rousing herself from her slumbers, she yawned, stretched, touched the long exploring roots of the oldest trees, and the ground shook; so too did the floor and ceiling.

It was only a small tremor but strong enough to bring a picture clattering from the wall. *'Panayia mou',* shrieked Erasmia, the comely wife of our patron Theodoros, over the sound of falling pans in the kitchen below. *'Ine o sismos* – an earthquake!' and in the garden of a neighbouring house a tethered mongrel strained on its chain and began to bark

'Happy birthday!'

hysterically. 'Happy Birthday,' I spluttered as a thin layer of dust settled on Maria's head, turning her blonde hair dirty white and making me choke, 'and many of 'em'. It was a dramatic start to the day, matched only a short while later by the entrance of Little Yanni.

'*Hronia pola!*' he yelled as in answer to his call we appeared at the top of the flight of stone steps leading to the courtyard where he stood cradling an antique shotgun. 'Many years!' he shouted and discharged both barrels into the air. '*Ne,*' seconded Papa Stylianos, ambling in his wake and producing a Beretta automatic from under his robes and doing likewise. '*Na zisate* – may you live!' '*Mana mou!*' screamed Erasmia clapping her hands to her ears and calling again on the Holy Mother. 'It is not enough that my best pot is broken by the earthquake that you have to try to bring down the heavens?' '*Mi milas!*' said Papa Stylianos benignly and proffering Maria a single mildewed rose in an empty retsina bottle, 'be quiet! It is after all her birthday.' '*Ne,*' cried Little Yanni reloading his firearm and pulling the triggers, 'bam boom!'

It was an eventful Friday on which the sun set. At six thirty that evening, two hours before it sank below the rugged hills, and crushed by the ample voluminous black-robed Stylianos, we crammed on to the bench seat of Little Yanni's Volkswagen van with himself at the wheel and snaked our way upward to Kakodiki. '*Kyrie Eleison,*' intoned Papa Stylianos using his walking-stick as a rifle and sniping through the open side window at everything that moved as we squealed around hairpin bends, '*kyrie eleison* and bam! bam!' He was in very good spirits. 'Ho! Ho! Ho!' he rumbled as narrowly we missed a hump-backed Quasimodo of a goatherd leaning upon his crooked stick and shepherding his flock of five. 'Ho! Ho! Ho!' 'Ha! Ha! Ha!' echoed Little Yanni in a minor key as two jack-booted old men sitting side-saddle on donkeys suddenly appeared in his windscreen, and crashed his gears. 'Tell me,' I asked, holding fast to Maria as a straying black dog with eyes dilated in terror leapt out of our path, and raising my voice above the revving engine, 'what are the names of your friends in Kakodiki?' 'Arati,' he shouted, changing gear again. 'I was at school with her. She has two daughters and a son of fifteen – a huge lad. *Ne*. He is a little *artsibutsi* you understand – a little mixed up. He is all right with the goats and olives but not much good in the classroom. *Ne*, he will be there, and so will her husband Nikos who is deaf – very deaf.' '*Ne*,' cried Papa Stylianos breaking off from his target practice, 'like Odysseus' sailors his ears are full of wax and one has to shout at him. But my God he can drink! How he can drink!'

Fifteen minutes later we shuddered to a halt on a slope outside Nikos' and Arati's *cafeneon*. '*Kalos! Kalos!*' called Arati waving to us from the doorway and wiping her hands on her apron as she came to greet us. 'Welcome! Welcome!' 'Yasu!' said Little Yanni as Papa Stylianos exited backwards from the van and guided us toward our hostess and effected introductions. 'But we are not staying now you understand?' '*Ne*,' said Papa Stylianos ponderously advancing to a chair on the veranda, 'they are going to church: indeed to three churches. And who knows,' he enquired as he took his seat and gave a benison to five white cats who with ramrod tails and twitching whiskers ran towards him, 'they may even light a candle for me. Ho! Ho!' 'But of course,' beamed Arati emptying a carton of day-old chicks into a low wire-netted cage and startling its six incumbent young partridges, 'but be back within the hour. Nikos should have returned by then from his goats.' '*Endaxi*,' said Little Yanni, and marshalled us into the van.

It was an interesting ecclesiastical tour. Each tiny oblong whitewashed chapel had a gently curving roof and a bell tower with a single bell over a severe rectangular entrance. The interior walls of each building were decorated with disfigured fading frescos of saints, sinners and anguised souls, and all were cluttered with pressed tin icons of arms, legs, hearts and eyes left by the afflicted faithful in the hope of eventual cure of their particular malaise. In each one we lit a candle, offered up a prayer and then marvelled at the preserved work of artists of five hundred years ago. But it was the last chapel which impressed us most.

From a panel to the left of the open sanctuary screen beyond which no woman is allowed, a life sized painting of the Virgin Mary, the All-Holy-One of Greek Orthodoxy, draped in robes of Prussian blue and crimson, stared impassively at us from an ornately scrolled golden throne. On her lap, her hands about Him, sat the Christ-child. But this was no cuddlesome innocent naked babe of the Umbrian School. Here was a miniature adult, a Holy Child who knew all the secrets of life and death, a worldly-wise Jesus already briefed about good and evil and the iniquities of mankind, and He looked uncompromisingly at us from His perch on His mother's knee.

High above the Virgin's head and the two seraphim attending her and close to a garish painting of Christ as God which sprawled across the blue curved ceiling, a pair of swallows nested on a ledge staining the wall and floor with their white and yellow droppings. Near the entrance and rising from the ground six grotesque Dantesque faces, their toothless mouths agape, howled in torment in the flames of eternal damnation, and between the depictions of Hell and Heaven, begrimed and crudely executed flights of arrow-riddled martyrs and others with blood spurting from decapitated shoulders floated upward to a cobwebbed Elysium.

Grey holes marked the places where the saints' eyes had been and I remarked upon them to Little Yanni. '*Ne*,' he said as I pointed to the empty sockets, 'that was the work of the Turks. Everywhere you understand, those barbarians gouged out the eyes.' '*Ne*,' I agreed, 'it was a sacrilegious act. But,' I said tentatively, 'I have heard that it was not only the Turks who did these disgusting things, that young Greeks and Cretans also picked away the sacred plaster and sprinkled it in wine as a love potion to entice women to their beds.'

Little Yanni looked aghast. 'And who has told you these things?' he husked disbelievingly. 'Who has fed you such lies?' 'A man in Heraklion,' I said, 'a tourist guide at Knossos.' 'Po! Po! Po!' exploded Little Yanni throwing his arms in the air and breaking the aura of reverence, 'a man from Heraklio? That explains it! Do you not know that all men from Heraklio are liars? And especially tourist guides? *Ne!* They are a different race! *Mana mou*, I would not trust one of them! Do you know what they would charge you for a *moussaka* in Heraklio . . .?' and snuffing out our candles he gestured towards the door. '*Ella pethia mou* – it is time we left.'

That evening was a merry one. After bellowed introductions to the afflicted and unwashed Nikos, a brawny, smiling, bald-headed unshaven man, smelling strongly of goat and with curling black moustaches which all but met his side-whiskers, we sat outside the *cafeneon* under a vine-covered canopy sipping *tsikouthia* and watching the day die until the cooling night air drove us in. Inside the grey-green painted room, its walls adorned with bottles, bandoliers and cartridge belts and other examples of the hill-villagers' way of life, an oscillating radio played *lyra* music. Across the terrazzo floor cluttered with chipped formica-topped tables, rush-seated wooden chairs and empty beer crates, Arati's backward boy, his head cupped in his hands, nasally accompanied the plaintive notes and picked his nose contemplatively. Next to him, oblivious of abstractions aural or visual, his grandfather read a newspaper, while Nikos, leaning upon a refrigerated cabinet piled high with bottled beers, bawled down the telephone to Athens.

'*Mana mou!*' he shouted crashing down the receiver and glaring at us, 'in the name of God why do some people mumble?' '*Scarsi!*' yelled Little Yanni picking up a fork and advancing upon him, 'shut up and clean out your ears with this!' '*Ne*,' said Papa Stylianos joining in the mockery, 'or wash them out with retsina.' 'Retsina?' bellowed Nikos, 'Only fools on the mainland drink retsina. *Ne!* And I have seen what it does to them you understand. It attacks their joints and makes them arthritic and they wake up with seeping eyes like wounded pines from the resin. *Ne! Sovara* – seriously. Now *tzikouthia* is another matter.' And reaching out for a bottle fitted with a rubber-tubed dispenser he stuck it into his ear. '*Endaxi!*' he shouted as the liquor trickled through his stubble. '*Tora ine kalitera* – now it is better. *Lipon,* well, where are your glasses? *Panda harumene!'*

Little by little the *cafeneon* filled. Bristled Yiorgos and Yannis, Manolises and Pavloses, shepherds, goatherds and workers from the oil presses next door *'yassued'* Arati and Nikos and then wandered to their accustomed seats. All greeted us warmly and all, when advised that it was Maria's birthday, wished her everlasting life and raised their glasses to her. Gradually, spearheaded by Nikos, the decibel level increased. Toasts rang out across the room, glasses clinked and bottles emptied as *kephi,* the spirit of goodwill, well-being and joy, embraced us all. Higher and higher rose the voices and thicker and thicker became the atmosphere. Fists fragmented twice-baked bread, a huge Graveira cheese was carved, fishes were flung on to the smoking central stove, grilled and then handed round like the distribution at Galilee, forks unequal to dealing with *brisola* – chops – from an outsize pig bent under pressure, and local red wine with a taste of sherry was poured from a widow's cruse.

'Ine kala?' inquired Papa Stylianos raising his voice above the hubbub and smacking a fish on the spine with the back of his fork and deftly removing the backbone. 'It is good?' *'Kataplicktiko!'* said Maria as he speared a morsel and offered it to her. 'Fantastic!' *'Ne,'* cried Little Yanni refilling our glasses and saluting them with his, 'did I not say we would have a fiesta? *Sisthireneos!'* *'Ne,'* repeated Papa Stylianos 'strength to everybody,' and he started to sing.

In the way that only a Cretan can, and with half-closed eyes searching the smoke-stained ceiling for inspiration, he sang a *mandinatha* – an instant improvisation of fifteen-syllable rhyming couplets set to a traditional tune – a conversation piece in song. His voice was baritone, beautiful and strong, and as the last lingering grace notes of his song died away, the company cried out. *'Ella! Ella! Ella!'* they chorused and repeating the last half of his final line, like ripples on a pool, each man in turn, even Nikos with his hand cupped behind his ear to catch the responses, picked up the theme and made his contribution. '*Ya!*' roared everyone as the sago ended and once again the glasses clinked and the celebrations continued. Songs in which we could join were sung, Little Yanni switched on a cassette player and danced to the *pentozali* – the quickest of all the Cretan dances – and then, as the tape ended, to wild acclamation a sweating Nikos and his son waving pump-action shot-guns over their heads rushed out through the door and emptied them into the canopy! '*Bravo!*' applauded one and all as vine leaves fell about their heads like confetti, 'more! more! more!'

It was a *feu de joie* to which we became accustomed. Cretans are born with the sound of gunfire in their ears and the smell of spent cartridges in their nostrils. From the cradle to the grave the gun is revered in the hills of Crete and daily the mountains echo to shots. No peasant is without at least one firearm and will blaze away at the sun and the stars if the *kephi* takes him, for guns are not only kept for hunting but for expressing joy and exuberance. We heard them at christenings, betrothals and weddings; at never-to-be-forgotten evenings in Azogires and Maza – hill villages where distances are measured not in terms of miles but in accordance with Cretan tradition in terms of the time the journey takes. On each occasion the fusillades rang out, disturbing the peace and frightening livestock, but it was on that night in Kakodiki that we were first introduced to the extravagences of Cretan fire-power.

We made a happy foursome when, brushing aside the out-stretched arms of sleep, we were bundled into Little Yanni's van in the small hours of the morning. '*Sto kalo!*' shouted Nikos embracing us sweatily and clanging the doors shut. 'Go to the good!' '*Episis,*' yelled Little Yanni, starting the engine, 'and you – if you can hear me! *Kali nichta!*'

The downhill journey home was a trifle erratic. Stray cats, rabbits and other fauna dazzled and bemused by our substand-ard headlamps caused Little Yanni to curse, swerve and brake abruptly, but Papa Stylianos blessed every one of them, sang all the way back and was still in good voice when we dropped him off at his house and received a final benediction from him.

Slowly the three of us walked back to the *pension* through the deserted, noiseless main street and halted outside it. The night was still, the air heavy with the scent of jasmine, and overhead the sky was pregnant with stars. The Wain of which Homer wrote hung low, its pointers guiding us to Polaris in the Little Bear, and to the west the sickle head of the Lion, which so legend has it was killed by Hercules and its skin fixed to the sky with diamond-studded nails, shone down upon a sleeping Paleochora. And as we looked, a meteor, glowing red as it vaporised, streaked across the sky.

'Ah,' said Little Yanni breaking the silence, '*ta telonia* – an air demon! *Ne*, my father would cross himself and say a prayer when he saw such things for they meant death for someone. *Ne*, that is what the old people believed and some still do in the hills.' 'And do you?' I asked him. '*Oche*,' he said, and laughed. 'You see Yanni *mou*, I *know* what that was. That was God saying *hronia pola* – many years – to Maria.' And he put his arm around her waist and squeezed it. '*Lipon*,' he said, 'it will soon be dawn. *Kalos hypnos pethia mou* – sleep well my children.'

Maria enjoyed two memorable consecutive birthdays in Crete, but fate denied her a third celebration. In the very early morning of the day before the event and with a crash which must have been measurable on the Richter scale, I fell backward down a flight of fourteen stone steps in our *pension*, fractured my head on the paved courtyard and, as it transpired, broke my back. It was a splendid production number and one which, suitably embroidered, was to enter the annals of Paleochoran folklore.

Bleeding profusely from my scalp and accompanied by Maria I was driven over an unmade road in an unsprung ambulance to the general hospital in Chania two hours distant. It was a salutary experience. Once there and ensconced in a wheelchair designed to cater for a Macedonian dwarf, I was zig-zagged into the outpatients department and examined first by a cigarette-smoking nurse whose finger-nails matched her rolled-down black stockings, and then by a similarly addicted doctor with an ill-fitting hairpiece and very thick glasses. Both allowed ash from their half-smoked cigarettes to fall into my open wound before the latter, sighing deeply after a final inhalation, stitched me up with the expertise of a novice crochet-worker. He then offered me two aspirin and suggested I returned to Paleochora. However, he continued, lighting a fresh cigarette from the stub of the other, if I were insured perhaps it would be advisable for me to go back to England as quickly as possible – and get a brain scan.

Hippocrates would not have been proud of him. Two hours later and aided by Maria and Nikos the ambulance driver, an admirable man with whom frequently we had kept company in Marko's *cafeneon* despite his appalling BO, carefully I was laid on my bed where I prayed for death. Next day I was stretchered back to Chania, flown feet first to Athens and then to hospital in England but not before most of the village had filed past my bed, weeping. As Maria remarked later, it was not unlike the lying-in-state of the Pope.

'*Thenbirazi*,' choked Little Yanni giving me a bottle of ouzo and kissing me on both cheeks, 'it could have been worse.' '*Ne*,' said Markos and Evangelina his wife, presenting Maria with a ripe goat's milk cheese and peering with prurient curiosity at my bandaged head, 'much worse.' '*Symphono*,' said Papa Stylianos bringing up the rear and giving me what in my dazed condition I assumed to be Extreme Unction, 'I agree. And Yanni *mou*, take heart! I do not think God wishes you to have *mezé* with Him just yet. You will, my friend return to us! *Endaxi?*' '*Endaxi*,' I slurred, 'OK.' '*Bravo!*' applauded Papa Stylianos. '*Ke bravo* Montgomery! All-right- yes!'

Papa Stylianos' optimism was justified. We did return to Paleochora; and will do so again, for that and other villages in south-west Crete have captured our hearts. But weeks after that trauma and when still restricted to the horizontal, I read and reread a message which he had sent to me. It was a quotation from Socrates.

'Remember,' the philosopher wrote, 'no human condition

154

is ever permanent; then you will not be overjoyed in good fortune, nor too sorrowful in misfortune.'

As I have said, Papa Stylianos is a remarkable man. But to cite once more the words of Homer: 'the Cretans are a singular people . . .'

Acknowledgements

Timsway Travel
Colin Murison Small Esq.